FINDING

YOUR INNER

BITCH

FINDING
YOUR INNER
BITCH

How to live an abundant and
wholehearted life

Pamela J. Maxson, PhD, ACC

Sol Searching Publishing

Sol Searching Publishing
Durham, North Carolina 27707

Copyright © 2019 by Pamela J. Maxson
All rights reserved. Published 2019
Printed in the United States of America

ISBN 978-1-7332897-1-9

Editor's note

This publication is not intended as a substitute for the advice of health care professionals.

The material in this book is intended for educational purposes only. No expressed or implied guarantee of the effects of the use of the recommendations can be given or liability taken.

Cover design and illustration by Clare Il'Giovine
Photo credit by Clare Il'Giovine

Dedicated to you, my reader. My dream is that we have a burgeoning revolution of discovered, excavated, released, nurtured, and celebrated inner bitches.

Table of Contents

I am not what has happened to me. I am what I choose to become.

– Carl Jung

If you read nothing else, read this!

Why Finding your Inner Bitch?

I have heard that one should write the book she needs to read. I have needed to read this book for a long time – when I was 13 and took comfort and solace in food; when I was 18, on the brink of starting college, and unsure of what I wanted in my life; when I was in graduate school and followed the path of least resistance. I needed this book when I was carrying my candy bar around to lose weight (Yes, totally illogical. Stay tuned to learn more), working on changing my thoughts, beliefs, actions, habits, life. I needed this book as a young mother and as a not-so-young mother. I need this book now.

So I am writing this book. For me. And I invite you to come along with me. I hope you find it meaningful. But this book is for me. This book is for my inner bitch. She needs to be heard. She knew what she wanted all along – at all those times I mentioned above. She was there, telling me. But I couldn't hear her for all the noise in my head. The noise from my noisy roommate. The noise from the media. The noise from years and years of expectations. The noise from internalized stories I held inside for too long.

Inner bitches and noisy roommates? All of us have both – each more or less developed. And we have to decide which to listen to.

What do I want from this book? I have listed a few things below – the first line is how I initially wrote it. Then I realized I wanted to personalize it, own it. I want you to own it as well.

I want women to realize they can express themselves without fear holding them back.

I want to realize I can express myself without fear holding me back.

I want women to live a fully authentic life.
I want to live a fully authentic life.

I want women to stop hiding who they really are, including from themselves.
I want to stop hiding who I really am, including from myself.

I want women to stop worrying about what everyone else thinks. Most of the time they aren't even thinking about you.
I want to stop worrying about what everyone else thinks. Most of the time they are not even thinking about me.

I want women to love their bodies and themselves for who they are.
I want to love my body and myself for who I am.

I want to empower younger women to assert themselves now.
I want to be empowered to assert myself now.

I want women to be empowered to speak up and to sit at the table.
I want to be empowered to speak up and to sit at the table.

I want to begin a revolution of women who know who they are and what they want and are skilled at asking for it.

I want to begin a revolution of women like me who know who we are and what we want and are skilled at asking for it.

I want to unleash the power of the hidden inner bitches inside so many amazing women. Women who have great ideas but who have buried those ideas under a lack of confidence or uncertainty.
I want to unleash the power of the hidden inner bitch inside my amazing self. I have great ideas but I have buried those ideas under a lack of confidence or uncertainty.

I want to counteract our societal messages about what it means to be a lady – I want to encourage women to be women.
I want to counteract our societal messages about what it means to be a lady – I want to encourage myself to be me.

I want to share my story of hiding my inner bitch which led to a myriad of issues, such as self-doubt, low self-esteem, anxiety, and eating disorders. And, most importantly, I want to share my story of finding and releasing her so she, and I, could thrive.

My inner bitch wants to write it. And I have learned it is best to listen to her.

A User's Guide to *Finding Your Inner Bitch*

A few years ago, I spent some time thinking about a personal mandala – a symbol – for my life. I began with a puzzle – full of bright, colorful pieces that would somehow fit together by the end of my journey. I loved parts of that analogy – it requires ingenuity, persistence, and reasoning to be solved. However, I wasn't fond of a puzzle being baffling or confusing. I viewed myself as evolving and developing, not difficult to understand.

Next I turned to a mosaic – a picture produced by arranging small colored pieces of hard material, often in a colorful, variegated pattern. The diverse elements come together to form a more or less coherent whole. I loved this. Yes, I have diverse elements that come together to form a more or less coherent whole. But then I realized a mosaic is static, created, and complete. I am still developing. I am still in creation. The mosaic was not quite me.

Ultimately, I chose the kaleidoscope for my mandala. A kaleidoscope is an instrument in which entering light creates colorful patterns, due to repeated reflection in the mirrors on the interior of the kaleidoscope. This results in a constantly changing set of colors, continually evolving as the shaft shifts. And, most importantly for me, the spaces between the colors create the visual pattern. It is the absence of color – the **pause** – that makes the colors stand out. I am continually shifting, with new patterns appearing as light is being reflected within me, and my colors becoming more vibrant as I pause.

Throughout *Finding Your Inner Bitch* (FYIB), you will find moments to pause interspersed. The pauses are the spaces between – where you will find exercises and prompts to help you begin to uncover, develop, and celebrate your inner bitch. It is these spaces in between that will create the colorful visual pattern of your life.

View the book as a journey, savoring the pauses, allowing your inner bitch to be your internal GPS. There are a few ways you can approach the pauses. You can go through the book from beginning to end, working on each pause as you come to it. You can read the whole book, keeping the pauses for after you have read everything. Or you can feel free to read and skip pauses if you want to dedicate more time than you have at the moment, coming back to them when you are able.

While the pauses are placed purposefully, each one stands alone. It is more important that you do the pauses at some point than that you do them in a particular way. This is your journey – make it your own.

Each pause is set apart by a kaleidoscope – an indicator that you are going to pause to make your colors shine.

You may want to pack for your journey, investing in a few provisions. A sketchpad, a journal, and some colored pens are good tools to bring along with you. Enjoy the shifting, the continually changing visual pattern of your life. For it is this shifting that is your life.

Finding Your Inner Bitch

Phase One: Discovering Your Inner Bitch

Chapter 1 Your Inner Bitch

Let me start by saying: "Bitch" is not a bad word. Bitch is loaded with negative connotations and imagery, and we live in a society that slings it around scornfully. I want to reclaim the term; to be a "bitch" is different than "being bitchy." Being bitchy is a state of grumpiness, however that may look. Being a bitch is different. To be a bitch is to be empowered. My declaration is: to be a bitch as a woman is equivalent to being a boss as a man. We may respect a boss, but we might not like when people are 'bossy'. Similarly, we can respect a bitch, but not like when people are 'bitchy'. If I were to consider the qualities of a bitch, the list would contain the following:

- **Smart**
- **Fiercely independent**
- **Able to leverage interdependence**
- **A leader**
- **A no-nonsense attitude**
- **Assertive**
- **Flexible**
- **Courageous**

It appears the qualities that make a woman a "bitch" are the very same attributes that make a man a success. When you meet a female who possesses those qualities, how do you feel? Comforted and secure? Uncertain and weary? Think of every female in a powerful position that you've encountered in your life. Your mother. A school principal. A colleague or a manager. Maybe even a friend or a total stranger. What do you think of when you think about a female Chief Executive Officer? A woman as a dominant figure in both male- and female-dominated arenas? A female as the next President of the United States? Do you think she is smart? Is she independent? Does she take charge and lead and not take anybody's crap? Does she have the courage to be doing whatever it is she set out to do? Do you see her as a bitch? We should, and we should embrace and celebrate those qualities. When a woman is engaged and excited; passionate and committed; utterly insatiable in her goals and aspirations, we need to celebrate and encourage her.

There have been many headlines about powerful women being called a 'bitch', and not with complimentary intent. And yet, these women are being called bitches for the very qualities that are revered in men. A reclaiming of the term, for ourselves and for society, will allow us to become our true selves, encouraging our strengths to shine, becoming leaders and creators, and guiding future generations of women to embrace their own inner bitches. If we don't reclaim the term, the hesitation to be strong, powerful, thoughtful women will continue and we won't leverage the strengths of half of our population.

A bitch is true to self, in tune with what she believes and wants, compassionate, sure of herself and her values, which allows her to more fully and generously hear others and live a genuine and fulfilled life.

Who is the inner bitch?

Who, then, is the inner bitch? She is the true you – the you that has been there all along but has perhaps intentionally gone into hiding or has been buried by internal and external messages about how we should behave. She is the internal you that is willing to stand up for yourself. The one who knows that an inner bitch is not a complaining, angry or unhappy woman. She is an empowered, thoughtful woman who is aware of what she needs and wants and knows how to ask for those things. She is a woman who knows that self-care is equally or more important than other-care; she is a woman who prioritizes herself, knowing that if she is a priority then everything else will fall into place; she is a woman who knows that standing up for herself and for others is appropriate; she is a woman who is fulfilled, who has taken the time to explore what she wants and is willing to make and implement plans to get there; and she is a woman who understands how her path, bumps and all, made her who she is and who has a vision for her path forward.

The unintentional (?) hiding of the inner bitch

Our society has unintentionally (perhaps) encouraged the hiding of the inner bitch through our socialization of girls into women. Little girls are often encouraged to be a lady; they are definitely not encouraged to be a bitch. Although I can see it now! My dream is that moms everywhere will be encouraging their daughters to be bitches – to say what they think in thoughtful, empowered ways. We have hidden generations of inner bitches through socialization, anti-bitch messages, the curse of busyness and dampening of feelings.

We unintentionally perpetuate societal rules about how girls should behave, even if we don't consciously believe them, because we are unaware of how powerful socialization is. We as women sometimes find it difficult to support other women who make choices that differ from our own. Perhaps this is because we are uncertain of our path, so we criticize others' decisions to feel better about our own. These conflicting messages send our inner bitches into hiding. And yet, if our inner bitches are involved in the decision-making, we will make the right choice for ourselves and allow others to choose their own way. All paths are meaningful. All paths are worthy. We would not need to be critical of others to make ourselves feel better if our choices were aligned with our true selves.

Why should we find our inner bitch?

Your inner bitch will help you live your most fulfilled, authentic lives. She will help you know what you want and how to work towards that while being compassionate and thoughtful. So you can step fully into our lives. Now. Not later. Not waiting until X or Y happens. No more slogging through your days to get to an elusive 'someday' when you can live your life and do what you want. That time is now. Your days are your lives. And you need to live them.

You have one life. Don't wait to live it. Who is the essential you? How can you express her? What is it that you want out of life? How can you live your best life? And if you live your best life, what are the amazing consequences? Who would be watching and learning from you? Who would benefit from this beyond yourself? We need the unleashed thoughts and power of all people.

Empowered women will make society stronger. Empowered women will cultivate empowered girls, ultimately facilitating diversity of thought, which is critical to improvement. It's a cycle either way – empowerment or silencing. Which do you want to choose? Without conscious awareness, we may reinforce silencing behaviors unintentionally.

We often act or don't act because we worry what other people might think. Many times others are not thinking about us in the way we think they are. We also do not need everyone to like what we say or do. It is wasted inner bitch silencing.

Imagine what the world would be like if women were whole. We would unleash our power, increase diversity of thought and action, with amazing ripple effects in friends, colleagues, students, children – both male and female.

The purpose of this book is to help women of all ages get in touch with who they are and encourage them to be confident sharing their true selves, to help them understand and embrace that they are worthy of being heard.

We want this for ourselves. For our friends. For our colleagues. For our daughters. For our granddaughters and those beyond who may not even be a thought yet.

How do we find her?

Finding her is a journey. In this book, we **discover, excavate, release, nurture,** and **celebrate.** The process is similar to trying on clothes – seeing what fits, and what feels good. Just because something fits our body doesn't mean it fits our soul. The process can be accompanied by growing pains. We can feel great exultation when we stand up for ourselves and walk away feeling empowered, albeit shocked at the same time. Particularly in the beginning of the journey, we may vacillate from "Wow! I can't believe I said that. Go me!" to "I can't believe I said that. Oh no!" within seconds. But over time we can learn to quiet the inner critic who has for years contributed to the silencing. And soon the 'Oh no's' will pass more quickly, allowing the 'Go me!' to flourish and grow.

Discovering your inner bitch

Discovering your inner bitch involves recognizing what you think after years of silencing and minimizing the amount of

17

space, physical or metaphorical, that you take up. It requires taking time for yourself, caring for yourself, putting yourself first, putting your oxygen mask on before you help others put on theirs. Breathe. Inhale. Exhale. Pause. Recharge.

Excavating your inner bitch

Excavating her requires some internal work – uncovering the stories we carry, rewriting those stories, stepping into our truth, being vulnerable in the right situations with the right people, taking risks, living "as if", rewarding ourselves, getting in touch with what we want and who we are. It involves surrounding ourselves with supportive team members, finding a tribe we trust and with whom we can be vulnerable, and letting our inner bitch shine as she feels ready.

Part of the process is quieting the constant, primarily negative, chatter of what I call the noisy roommate, sometimes referred to as the inner critic. We hear thousands of statements a day from this roommate –from "buckle your seatbelt" and other innocuous messages, to shaming messages that seem like they are shouted from the rooftop. Even as I write this, my noisy roommate is stirring up trouble for me, distracting me with self-doubt.

If we can change our thoughts and quiet our minds for even small chunks of time, we will be barraged by fewer negative messages and be less likely to believe them.

It is important to recognize the source of these internal statements – is it noise from your noisy roommate? If it is a negative message, then it likely is. Combatting the noisy roommate takes practice and committed energy but can save energy in the long run. Being aware of the source of the message allows one to acknowledge and then dismiss them. Eventually quieting that roommate will allow inner peace as well as clarity around what your real thoughts are. What your inner bitch truly wants to say. Silencing that noisy roommate is not only acceptable, it is appropriate and necessary. We can't let the negative faceless messages affect our decisions and actions.

Many of the messages from the noisy roommate originate in the stories we hold on to throughout our life. Stories from long ago – stories which have become emblazoned on our hearts – stories which are no longer relevant but which still hold great power over us. We will uncover these stories and rewrite those that no longer work for us, excavating our inner bitch from these layers in the process.

Releasing your inner bitch

Once you have found your inner bitch, how do you let her out? How do you express her? Your inner bitch may initially be fledgling – desperately wanting to fly but needing to develop the thicker feathers necessary for flight. She may be hesitant to show herself and you may have difficulty hearing her. This is an incremental process with small successes and deliberate habit changes. We will explore deliberate and intentional steps to release her, including choosing safe situations in which to practice. This may also involve finding areas where you can explore, including new activities and new friends, in addition to relying on your tribe that you intentionally develop.

Nurturing your inner bitch

Nurturing our inner bitch means embracing our faces, hair, bodies for the beauties that we are. Wrinkles, earned; cellulite, natural; frizzy hair, expressive. Who we are does not need to be molded, shaped, flattened, squeezed. It means saying 'World, I am me. And I am here.' Shame, displeasure, and discontent with our appearances are a waste of time and energy. They are a distraction at best and a way to usurp our power at worst. Feeling not "good enough" can make a person afraid or unwilling to sit at the table and speak up. Not feeling "attractive enough" can discourage someone from drawing attention to herself.

Silencing. Primping. Measuring up. Cultural messages covertly encourage girls/women to bury their inner bitch – to not let it fully develop – to not argue their point – to not speak over their peers and adversaries. Where are the messages coming from? Pay attention to how you feel – physically, emotionally, spiritually – when you hear these messages. Do they make you feel small? Powerful? Energized? Drained?

How do you feel at the beginning of the day? "Got my shit together – these heels are killin' it." At the end of the day – "OMG, I've got to take off this bra – and my shoes are killing me!"

Nurturing your inner bitch means choosing what is right for you, and her. It means taking care of you, prioritizing you, and listening to your own needs and wants.

Celebrating your inner bitch

Throughout this book, we will be finding and releasing your inner bitch. Equally important is allowing her to thrive by celebrating her (and thus you). When you have finished an exercise or when you feel the glimmer or radiance of your inner bitch, pause and acknowledge her. Celebrate your successes, each step of the way.

Beginning the journey

I'm excited to begin this journey with you. Let's get started!

Pause: Mind Mapping

Mind mapping is a technique that can be used to think about an issue, to delve deeply by letting the right side of your brain take over. For left-brained, analytical people like me, mind mapping is a great tool that encourages creativity without being intimidating. I don't have to come up with something mind-blowing, just some circles and lines – with a connection between them that may or may not be obvious. Sometimes my mind maps are simply balloons in the air with no connection. Other times the connections are strong and the mind map looks very organized. The only rule is that there are no rules.

I have used mind mapping to help me figure out problems, make decisions, and connect with my inner bitch. I have mind mapped who I was as a child – the influences on me, my beliefs that were instilled in me by others, my activities, my roles. I have mind mapped who I am now – the roles I fill, the traits I possess, the beliefs I hold. I have mind mapped the stories that I have carried with me, often long beyond their utility. I have mind mapped my to-do list, particularly when I am feeling overwhelmed, organizing my jumbled thoughts into a visual representation. Many of my clients like the creative aspect of mind mapping and use it often in their journaling.

You don't need any special tools for mind mapping, but I like good paper and colored pens. These things remind me of the beginning of the school year – and a blank sheet of paper offers such promise. I like high quality multi-media sketchbooks, but any paper, even a napkin in a pinch, will do. Because I am not particularly artistic, I grasp any opportunity I can to use cool supplies.

Mind mapping is an excellent tool to use when you want to reframe a situation or think about something in a way that is different than you normally would. Do not judge yourself when you do this – put whatever comes to mind on your map. You want your mind to be able to process without constraints. You can review it later. Sometimes connections and thoughts appear when and where you least expect them.

Exercise. Here are some mind mapping prompts to get you started. Put yourself or the question in the middle and draw bubbles around the main bubble (containing you or the question). Then draw bubbles off of each of the individual bubbles as your thoughts progress. If you would like a visual example, many can be found online.

What are you excited about? What is energizing you?

- Put yourself in the middle, and add your thought bubbles around you.
- Only draw lines to yourself if you can do anything about the situation.
- Leave those items over which you have no control unconnected to you.
- Then, from each thought bubble, jot down some potential ways you can act on that idea or concern.
- Put the central issue in the middle
- Think about all of the aspects of the issue

- Then be creative about how to act on those things. Potential solutions or components can be connected to the second level bubbles.

Other prompts for you to explore:

- What do you like to do for fun?
- How do you spend your time?
- What would you do if you could do anything at all, with no concern for money?
- What makes you happy?
- When do you feel joy?
- What are your personality characteristics and how do they show up in your life?

Pause: Who am I?

Many things influence who we are and who we become. In this exercise, explore who you are. When you meet someone, what do you say about yourself? How do you define yourself? This exercise has three parts. **It is important to do them in order so you allow your inner bitch to come out of hiding.** You can do this exercise any way you would like – mind map, journal, list, sticky notes. Be creative in your expression.

Work on this exercise in parts, finishing one part before moving on to the next since they build on each other.

Part One. Who am I?

When you meet someone, what do you say about yourself? What words do you use to define or describe yourself?

Part Two. Who am I without my Roles?

Now consider who you are without using any role definitions (wife, mother, sister, daughter, friend, etc.). What are your characteristics, values, goals, dreams? You may have touched on these in part one, but feel free to repeat them. Each part of this exercise will expand the picture of who you are, excavating and finding your inner bitch.

Part Three. Furthering my Understanding

You may have found the previous exercises difficult because you ran out of things to say. We do not often give ourselves the gift of space and time to contemplate who we truly are. The following questions will deepen your understanding of who you are and what you like, unveiling your complexity and multidimensional wonder.

Think about your tendencies and preferences. When do you feel most content and whole? Learning these things about ourselves is an essential way to know what we need.

While these questions appear to be either/or, your answers may reflect the flexibility of the question – it depends on the situation. And you may be somewhere in between. There is no right or wrong answer. There is only you.

Consider each of the following questions.

- o Do you like to be alone or surrounded by people?
- o Do you prefer quiet spaces or lots of stimulation?
- o Do you like to spend time inside or in nature?
- o Do you prefer sweet or savory foods? When you want a snack, which do you lean toward?
- o What textures do you like or dislike in foods? Crunch, silkiness, chewiness?
- o Are you a morning or a night person? When do you feel the most energized?
- o What situations or people that make you feel alive?
- o What are the things that make you feel whole?
- o When do you feel most centered?
- o What is your favorite time of day?

When you have thought more deeply about who you are, you can use this information to work with your tendencies and preferences to more often put yourself in situations when you are more 'you', where you feel more aligned with what works best for you. We can't always avoid situations which are not synergistic with our true selves, but we can minimize their frequency.

We can use our highest energy points (time of day, location, surroundings, etc.) to maximize our potential. When we leverage our tendencies and preferences, we naturally compound our effectiveness and well-being.

Reflect on Part Three. How can you maximize your potential to be your most aligned self? What can you begin to do more of or less of to be your true self? Are there people you want to see more or less frequently? Do you want to change your routine so you are able to reflect and do your best work while you have the highest energy? Capture your reactions and thoughts about this exercise in the journal you packed for your journey.

Chapter 2: Development and the Inner Bitch

Our life offers many points of inflection and vulnerability, where the inner bitch may find safety and flourish or anticipate risk and hide. When we look at development across the life course, we can see the intentional and unintentional development of the inner bitch. There are times when the inner bitch would naturally thrive and others when she would naturally be dormant. What influences her development? How do we, as parents, teachers, friends, and individuals, unintentionally subdue her, putting her on a path of remaining hidden to varying degrees? How do internal and external influences make us who we are?

Path to Self-Actualization

Abraham Maslow, a 20th century psychologist, was at the forefront of positive psychology with his interest in how humans could become all they could possibly be. He created a hierarchy of needs[1], describing how our needs motive our behavior. The ultimate goal is self-actualization – the process through which we become our best, utilizing our talents and skills in meaningful ways, taking time for introspection and growth. I believe that **self-actualization is the full expression of our inner bitch**. Each of the other needs in the hierarchy lay the foundation for self-actualization. The inner bitch can wither or flourish through the meeting of these needs.

Maslow's Hierarchy of Needs[1]

The most basic level is our physiological needs – food, water, sleep. Meeting these needs is paramount for optimal health and well-being. While many of us are fortunate and have the financial ability to have our basic needs met, we don't always meet them in ways that best suit us. We may not eat in ways that allow our body to thrive, consuming too much sugar or not enough fruits and vegetables. Or we may not get enough sleep due to work/family obligations or watching too much television. There is a difference between meeting a need for survival and meeting one to ensure optimal performance.

The second level is safety and security, with varying levels of meaning. The most basic is having a safe place to live, financial security, and protection from illness and accidents. How we measure these attributes differs. A person may feel their home or their bank account may have to be bigger and better in order to meet this need. Then we begin dabbling in the 'esteem' level of needs (4th level). The same items that can provide safety and security can also be superficial or outward measures of one's worth.

The third level is love and belonging. Belonging may be more accurately described as a pillar that goes through the hierarchy, as a person seeks belonging through all levels.

The desire for love and belonging can be a motivator for the hiding of the inner bitch. One becomes afraid that others will not love or accept her for who she really is, including her assertive, seemingly contrary parts, so she stops sharing those parts of her, silencing her true self in exchange for the hope of love and belonging. Perhaps not a conscious choice – rather it may be reinforced by family and society. When children are young, parents, teachers, and other agents of socialization are concerned with teaching them to follow the rules, become good citizens, and behave appropriately. All valiant goals, but they can come with a cost if the inner bitch is buried in the process.

Love and Belonging throughout the Hierarchy[2]

If all three levels of needs are adequately met, then esteem, the fourth level, becomes important. I believe, however, that even those individuals who do not have their basic needs met desire to feel good about themselves. Yes, we have the luxury of focusing more on our esteem if those more basic needs are met, but it is likely that esteem also runs through the hierarchy to some degree. The esteem need reflects the desire to be respected by others, to feel worthy, to be appreciated for who we are and what we have done. The esteem needs are critical in understanding why the inner bitch may flourish or whither. Those individuals who are able to get their esteem needs met feel good about themselves, have a strong sense of confidence in what they are doing, and are more likely to accept risk as part of life.

Those whose needs are not met may feel a lack of confidence, lower self-esteem, and allow fear to motivate their behavior. If the inner bitch has been allowed to express herself and guide decisions and behavior, esteem needs will likely be met, because one will be showing her true self to others. When her true self is nourished, nurtured, safe, and accepted, she will more likely feel worthy and respected. Her lens on life will be crystal clear, not clouded by fear.

The highest level, the top of the hierarchy, is self-actualization. In my view, a person does not become self-actualized. Rather one has a self-actualizing perspective, which motivates self-awareness and guides her behavior to allow her to become the best she can be, maximizing her potential. She will fully engage her talents and potential. To me, self-actualizing is a state where the inner bitch is fully expressive and occupies one's whole body, rather than a small spot deep in the recesses of one's heart. Self-actualization allows us to be who we are; it does not require us to change to please others. Maslow said, "What a man can be, he must be[3]." He did not say – what others think a man can be, he must be.

Maslow's hierarchy of needs offers perspective on why we behave in certain ways. Depending on what need we are trying to meet, we choose to behave in different ways. For example, clothing can satisfy a basic need and it can also meet a belonging and esteem need. One will choose differently depending on which need she is trying to meet. The needs are not mutually exclusive; you can meet more than one need at a time.

Needs will be more fully met if the inner bitch is able to stay present and vital. If she is hidden, your needs will not be met in the most optimal way. You may be motivated to belong by hiding your true self, or you may be motivated to spend more than you want to achieve belonging and esteem. And the only way to begin self-actualizing is to begin excavating your inner bitch. That's excellent – you are in the self-actualizing process by reading this book!

Pause: A Childlike View: Past, Present, Future

While we explore how we can be our best selves, sometimes we need to look back to get a clearer view of now. Numerous clients, students, friends, and colleagues have expressed they have no idea what their passion is, what they would find fulfilling to pursue, or even what they might do for fun. It is easy to lose those ideas about ourselves in the busyness of our lives. We can get lost in the pragmatic, the path to our next accomplishment, the daily to-do list. I am struck by how pervasive this feeling is. I hear it from 18 year olds, 30 year olds, 40 year olds, 50 year olds, and so on. We become so successful making and implementing plans that we sometimes lose our sparkle, our ability to think about what we really love to do.

This exercise will help you think about what you loved to do as a child, providing insight into what you might want to incorporate into your present life and continue to work toward in the future. You can build on this exercise to help you add more fun to your life, think about a career change, build new friendships, reignite old relationships, and more.

Exercise. Ask yourself the questions listed below. You may not have answers for all of them, and you may think of additional questions that are relevant for you.

Write down, draw, photograph, capture in whatever way you prefer all of the things that come to mind. I like what I call mind bubbles for this exercise. Mind bubbles is like mind mapping but without the connections and mapping component. It is a free-flowing capture of your thoughts in a judgment-free way. This is a foundational exercise on which later exercises will build. And you may also find that you return to this exercise repeatedly as you learn more about yourself.

Allow yourself to be childlike in this exercise. I encourage you to do this over a few sessions, in different places. This may take some time as you reflect on your past. If you are feeling particularly adventurous, engage in some of the activities you enjoyed as a child. Play in the mud, finger paint, get your hands dirty, wade in streams, splash in puddles. These activities may engage your mind in new ways. And they are fun!

Questions:

- What did I love to do as a child?
- How did I spend my free time?
- What kinds of toys did I like?
- What did I like to do with others? By myself?
- What did I want as a child?
- Were there activities I repeatedly asked to do?
- With whom did I like to spend time? Why?
- When I was a child and looked into my future, what did I see? What did my days look like?

Eight Stages of Man (and Woman)

Developmental psychologist Erik Erikson delineated eight stages of life[4] through which we develop. Socialization and expectations influence how we move through these stages, consequently affecting the development and potential hiding of the inner bitch.

Trust vs Mistrust: During infancy (ages 0-1 years), we begin to learn whether we can trust others to care for us, be responsive, and meet our needs. Parents and caregivers who respond sensitively and predictably will build the child's trust. Without knowing it, we often begin differentially reinforcing boys and girls during this stage, reacting more positively to boy infants who are loud and boisterous than to girl infants. We are more likely to pick up and cuddle a girl, quieting her, while we are more enthusiastic with boys who squeal. Infant girls learn early that quiet is better than loud. While not necessarily affecting the trust vs mistrust conflict, this can influence the development of the inner bitch's voice.

Autonomy vs Shame and Doubt: Toddlerhood (ages 1-3 years) is sometimes called the "terrible twos", because children are trying out a new-found independence garnered through increased physical and cognitive abilities. This age group is characterized by wanting to do things themselves, with their favorite phrase some variation of "me do." This is a delightful stage of discovery, new-found abilities, increased independence, and feelings of empowerment and confidence. Parents who are able to allow independence within safe boundaries help the child gain autonomy.

How do we nurture/quiet the inner bitch during this stage? Do we reinforce boys and girls differently as they try new and daring activities? Do we hold girls closer to us, subconsciously withholding encouragement for physical, risky behaviors, like climbing on short walls, jumping from curbs, splashing in puddles? Do we unintentionally instill a greater sense of fear, a hesitation to take risk at such an early age? If so, it is not entirely our own fault. We have been conditioned over years to protect and nurture girls and to encourage boys to be strong and brave.

The dichotomy of when we instill doubt and when we encourage autonomy for boys and girls is striking. We instill doubt in girls when they try something physical and daring. We instill doubt in boys when they express emotions or pain. At an early age, we tell boys to "brush it off", "man up." We are more likely to rush to little girls when they fall, accompanying our comfort with messages such as, "See, that is what happens when you do things like that," further instilling hesitancy and caution. We facilitate the initial hiding of the inner bitch, encouraging her to be afraid of the world and turn to safety.

Children are figuring out how they fit into the world, amidst its expectations, and deciding what they are going to choose to battle with their burgeoning autonomy. We readily equip boys for this battle, often allowing them to be more defiant, even encouraging them to challenge our rules and positively reinforcing them when they do.

What would happen if we equipped girls with capes and encouraged them to try out their newly found physical prowess? Jumping from curbs, splashing in puddles, digging in the dirt. What would happen if we allowed boys to cry and express their pain and fear? Perhaps we would allow both boys and girls more time and freedom to figure out more of who they are, without the limitations of our societal and cultural gender expectations.

Toddlerhood was likely a long time ago for you and only a vague memory, if that. Observe how toddlers are encouraged, reinforced, and discouraged in their activities. Most parents, myself included, often engage in subtle and mostly unintentional gender variation in our parenting, because we have been socialized according to gender expectations. If you are doubtful that this occurs, think about what happens when you find out someone is expecting a baby. The first question often is "Do you know if it is a boy or a girl?" Why do we ask this? Because the moment we know the answer, we develop a trajectory for that child's life in our head, and we begin to predict what parenting will be like for our friend. If we did not have differing expectations, the question would not arise. One trip to the card section at Target will demonstrate the stereotypes that society has embraced. And this is before the child is born. The toy section, the clothes section, the book section – all continue to weave the thread of gender through our tapestry of existence.

Initiative vs Guilt: Children (ages 3-5 years) now have increased cognitive abilities that allow them to make and carry through plans. However, their plans are not always well thought out with regard to consequences. Children in this stage are not cognitively astute enough to think all the way through to what it might mean if the plan is implemented. The classic example is Dennis the Menace and Mr. Wilson's prize roses. Dennis is very thoughtful and wants to give his mother a flower to show her how much she means to him. So Dennis goes to Mr. Wilson's prize rose garden with his scissors and cuts his mom a rose. Of course, while Dennis's mom is happy with the flower, she is chagrined and embarrassed when Mr. Wilson points out the unintentional destruction of property. Dennis thought of a plan, was able to carry it out, but failed to think through the consequences, bringing the wrath of Mr. Wilson.

What does this have to do with our inner bitches? We are differentially rewarded for the initiation and implementation of plans, even when we are only 3 years old. And we are also differentially sensitive, with some of us repeatedly covering our inner bitches. We were more in tune with wanting to please others, deferring to our parents, teachers, and friends. We often were trying to figure out what others thought and felt, likely due to societal messages, and putting our own desires second to others.

This is not a diatribe against socialization and culture. But it is critical that we are aware of our implicit and unintentional teachings – what are we teaching that we don't mean to teach. What have we accepted without challenging? What have we adopted and begun doing without even being aware of it? So much of what we do and believe is on autopilot. Being aware of our stories, our choices (conscious or subconscious), and their consequences are important components of reigniting our own fires and fanning the fires of the little girls we may be nurturing.

Industry vs Inferiority: Ah, the middle childhood years (ages 6-12 years) – a time when children are focused on learning and improving skills, figuring out where they fit in with regard to their abilities and how they compare to others. We begin realistically evaluating our abilities. During our amazing younger years (ages 3-5), we are invincible, we are the best at everything, and it is okay if everyone is the best. We are cognitively blessed during those preschool years to not be able to detect the incongruity in the belief that I am the best tree climber and Joey is too. Alas. We develop cognitively at the same time we are developing our fine motor skills and our hand-eye coordination. As we finesse our skills, our brain is also beginning to pull out the inconsistencies in previous thought patterns. There cannot be two bests, inevitably leading to the sense of inferiority.

Perhaps it is unfortunate that Erikson used the word "inferior." But I think we may have given the word another meaning in this context. Inferior means lower in ability. And we are all lower in ability compared to others on some things. And we are higher in ability on others. But we have attached an alternate meaning to the word as well – lower in status. And that bothers us. So we developed ways to battle this natural progression of development by artificially/superficially boosting self-esteem, such as participation trophies, alphabetical assignment of student of the week, and elimination of class rankings and valedictorians, to name a few.

There is a whole generation (possibly two) of parents that is cringing as they read this. And one of those generations is mine. We are the self-esteem parenting generation. Our initial thought was "How does this affect how you feel about yourself? That must hurt your self-esteem. Quick, let's give everyone a trophy." We are also the generation that began the revolution against teachers using red pens, claiming that a corrected school paper covered in red pen damages a child's self-esteem.

(I believe it is not the actual color of the pen – it is the tendency of teachers to overcorrect and over-comment, boldly suggesting that the child's work is not sufficient, not quality, not worthy. This tendency contributes to the hiding of the inner bitch. If a child repeatedly receives feedback that demonstrates his/her lack of ability and quality of work, then why would the child be motivated to express him/herself? Perhaps we could begin focusing on what was done well, what was amazing about the child's work, and suggest a few ways to make it better. And then ask for a revision. We do not need to accept low quality work, but maybe we need to redefine our expectations and our goals in learning. Do I want 25 papers that look exactly like I, as the teacher, would write it? Or do I want 25 students who are learning to express themselves and their views in meaningful and articulate ways? Which would, consequently, lead to a cadre of self-confident, expressive inner bitches. And the poor red pen could continue its valiant work.)

As children figure out what their strengths are in comparison to others, they begin to realize that they are indeed "inferior" in some areas as well. This is a good thing despite our initial emotional reactions. In an ideal world, we would learn as children that we are all different, and our unique abilities work beautifully together. And we can build on our strengths, getting better at our natural tendencies, helping us in the long run as we figure out what we love to do and what we want to contribute to the world through our work. Instead, we focus on our weaknesses. We focus on what needs to be bolstered – we focus on the many red markings on the paper. What was done incorrectly? Why did you get a C along with your five A's? How can you improve your lowest score? A weakness-based strategy diverts our efforts and energies away from our strengths. And it results in many people feeling uncertain and displeased with themselves. And then we need trophies for all!

Consequently, we unintentionally foster a tidal wave of young adults who do not know their strengths, are uncertain of how to find their passion, and are overwhelmed at the herculean task of figuring it all out. I encounter these young adults in droves. And these feelings of angst and uncertainty can often be traced back to this time period, the period of becoming industrious contributors to our society. The time during which we are rewarded and reinforced for our accomplishments. Some of us grab on to these accolades and begin to internalize the strong desire to achieve and exceed expectations. Others of us bury our strengths underneath our weaknesses, which we are tasked to bolster. And some do both – working hard to exceed expectations and achieve in the areas where we have shown some promise while minimizing the talents that may not have the opportunity to shine in the traditional academic/social settings.

But either way, the inner bitch may shrink, deferring to social expectations. Our focus on the inferior influences us in unintended ways. We fear making mistakes or taking a risk. We lack understanding and appreciation of our uniqueness. We are unable to make a free-flowing list of our strengths but are quick to make the parallel list of our weaknesses. We fear that even our strengths are weak in relation to others' strengths. We are stumped when we are asked what we want to do with our lives. Or we answer in the way that we have learned gets us positive reactions.

I hear young adults repeatedly say they decided on a particular career path (namely doctor, lawyer, or engineer) because of the responses they received from adults when they were younger. And they consequently stopped exploring other potential paths. They prematurely entered a path that they are now uncertain they want to follow. But I am relieved when I hear the uncertainty in young adults. I am saddened when I hear the same message from older adults who have followed that career path and are now realizing they have climbed the wrong ladder.

Identity vs Role Confusion (ages 13-21 years). Teenage angst. Teenage rebellion. Teenage wasteland. Parents may receive condolences when their children turn 13. The magic adolescent years. What changes between 12 and 13? Nothing really. And yet, 13 is a landmark birthday. One begins the transition period to adulthood. Although in our current time period, this is less true than previously. Our transition to adulthood is much longer, with the advent of longer educational careers and a financial environment which favors postponing leaving the parental nest.

Erikson claimed this time period is when individuals try on different identities, challenge previously accepted beliefs, and develop a sense of self. This may be associated with a separation from parental views, which can be temporary, a slight shift, or a radical departure. This may be why parents have trepidations about this time period. Their previously agreeable children are developing minds of their own, challenging what they had previously easily accepted. Cognitively, adolescents are gaining the ability to speculate, hypothesize, and think abstractly, all of which allows them to project themselves into the future, trying on identities to see how they fit.

Ideally, this is a time when the inner bitch would flourish. She would be encouraged to try on her metaphorical clothes and see what she likes. But, it's not that easy. Instead, we are so busy worrying about what our peers think, how we can fit in, and how we can be like everyone else, that we sometimes purposely hide our inner bitches during adolescence. Because while our developmental task may be to figure out who we are as individuals, our social environment asks the complete opposite of us. Be like the rest of us; don't stand out; blend in; wear what everyone else wears. Our cognitive abilities may be developing, but it comes with a sense of egocentrism[5] that makes us feel like the world is watching us, albeit not in a good way. We believe in an imaginary audience that is watching every mistake we make and ridiculing us along the way. And, unfortunately, the imaginary audience isn't always imaginary. We sometimes deflect our own insecurities by finding someone else to ridicule, and the cycle continues.

This is a challenging time of life. We are uncertain about who we are. Our bodies are doing things we don't fully understand. Our emotions are playing pinball within us. Academic, parental, and societal pressures are increasing. Our future is bearing down on us. The last thing we want is to be the center of unwanted attention. And yet we simultaneously crave it. We want to be noticed. We need to be acknowledged, to know we are important. But we fear it. We are ambivalent. So we hide our idiosyncrasies, the things that actually make us fantabulous, in order to be like everyone else. We hide our awesomeness.

And sometimes we hide behind undesirable behaviors. We drink; we smoke; we use drugs; we develop eating disorders; we overindulge in social media; and so on. And these behaviors may have long-lasting consequences. Because we don't know how to handle the insecurity, the questioning, and the pressure, we turn to self-placating behaviors. As a society, we don't encourage individuals to show their areas of being "inferior." We are to put on a strong, secure, confident persona to demonstrate our worth and our meaning. And yet – we lose our true identity, we ignore who we really are, we fear the questioning that is so important during this time period. We are not encouraged to try new things, skills or talents that may be positive additions to our lives. Rather than allowing our inner bitch to experiment with Goth, torn jeans, or bright, awesome colors, we bury her in others' expectations.

When older adolescents arrive in the college classroom, they do not readily ask questions. They are hesitant to stand out or disagree with each other. The classroom is ideally a judgment-free zone, where they are allowed to express their views, their experiences, their beliefs – their selves – without fear of judgment. Teachers may have to foster that zone by creating a safe space through formal class guidelines.

How ironic that we need to consciously make the college environment a space to allow vulnerability– a space of intellectual discourse where students may actually disagree with one another without fear. Where students learn to have differing views and still be able to hear one another, truly hear what someone has to say. And slowly, over the semester, inner bitches may emerge, regardless of gender.

A transition is occurring when adolescents move from trying desperately to fit in to being confused about who they are. It may appear like they are going backwards as they enter this state of confusion, but this questioning is a progression towards maturity. It is as if their shell around their real self begins to fall off during this time period – at least for those who go through it successfully. Those who grasp on to the shell, to the safety of certainty, are at risk of the shell hardening so much that if it does fall off later, it will crash as it hits the ground.

Identity Development. Understanding how identity forms can help us understand how we became who we are, how our decisions and challenges added layers to our identity, as well as how we can best help others successfully navigate their identity journey. Clinical and developmental psychologist James Marcia[6] presented a model of **identity achievement** characterized by whether an individual has questioned identity (conflict) or committed to aspects of identity (commitment). Identity formation flows through four states (diffusion, foreclosure, moratorium, and achievement). These states are not a continuum; people can go back and forth or skip one state entirely.

	No Commitment	Commitment
No Conflict	Diffusion	Foreclosure
Conflict	Moratorium	Achievement

James Marcia's Identity Statuses[6]

When an individual is in late childhood or early adolescence, she often has not questioned her identity, at least beyond the ubiquitous question of what she wants to do with her life thrown at her by hovering adults. She has beliefs, values, and roles without question or conscious acceptance or commitment (**diffusion**). In diffusion, there have been no "decisions" yet, no moments of choice, when one decides "this is who I am."

Foreclosure is when one prematurely chooses an identity, when a decision is made without questioning or active deliberation. This often happens with career paths – as mentioned previously, decisions to become a doctor or lawyer are often met with positive reinforcement so one can easily become convinced that is the desired direction. This also happens regarding politics or religion. One unquestioningly decides to follow a particular path – usually because of others such as parents, teachers, peers - without moments of "conflict," confusion or questioning. The individual is choosing without conflict.

This is often only temporary – how temporary depends on how in touch the individual is with her inner bitch and how encouraging her environment is toward change. If she is not aware of what she really wants or believes, developing her identity may be more challenging. She may feel firm in her beliefs, but her life may not be synchronous with what is deep inside her. She will not be living her best life. She may be living the life she believes someone else or society wants her to live. The tragedy is when that influential someone else doesn't truly care or feel strongly about it. Our earlier influences can be so powerful that they come along with us for the ride, often without our awareness unless we take the time to excavate our inner bitches.

Not everyone goes through foreclosure, although many of us do in some areas of our lives, at least for a little while. The next state is **moratorium,** a time of exploration. To move successfully through the identity process, girls need to feel free to question who they are and how they fit in to the world. Essentially, they need their inner bitch to be alive and kickin'. An individual is exploring who she is, trying things on for size, deciding what feels right. This may be the time when a young woman is experimenting with religions or career paths. She may feel that her peer group needs to be modified. She may become an activist for social change. And she may change monthly, weekly, or even daily. While she may appear like sea grass in the wind, fluctuating as the breeze changes, this is a healthy state to be in as she is actively working on who she is. The more receptive her environment (family, peers) is to these changes and the more aware she is of what fits, the easier this process will be. This can be confusing for the young woman as she may flit to and fro; allowing her inner bitch the space and freedom to explore will facilitate understanding of who she is, along with the accompanying beliefs, values, desires, and goals.

To my readers who are parents (or who will be someday):

47

the irony is that parents who fight against or are uncomfortable with the exploration may actually prolong the process. Parents who are willing to facilitate, or tolerate if need be, this exploration allow the individual the freedom to make her own decisions and achieve her own identity.

Admittedly, for parents this can be a challenging time. Be flexible and open to the change you see within your daughter (unless it involves danger to herself or others). She wants blue hair this week? Ok. She wants red hair next week? Ok. Eventually she will figure it out. And she may be subconsciously or consciously watching your reaction to her choices as she explores. The less you react to any particular identity she tries on, the more you will allow her to find what fits her rather than encourage her to make choices based on your reaction.

What a gift that is to her and her inner bitch. Loving her no matter what, showing her approval unconditionally, knowing that somewhere in that exploration is the core of who you know her to be – all of that is the greatest gift a parent can give a child. Being with her during the wind shifts, whether breeze or gale, and helping her however you can (e.g., helping fund some of the exploration, driving her to the grocery store to buy the sugar free Kool-Aid to dye her hair) will let her know that this exploration is safe and she can rely on you to stand by her while she is connecting with and allowing her inner bitch to flourish into who she is meant to be. AND at the same time, rely on your own tribe to help you through this time. Your inner bitch also needs to be heard – but not necessarily by your daughter. This is the time to garner support from other inner bitches – grown-up inner bitches preferably.

The culmination of the exploration, the questioning, the shifts in hair color, is **identity achievement**. Achievement happens after questioning and deciding. Remember that we have multiple facets of our identity – career, spiritual, family, political, gender, etc. A young woman may achieve identity in some areas more quickly and easily than in others. Identity is a process, not a product. And with every life transition, identity shifts. New job? Who are you in that job? Changing family status? Identity needs to be reevaluated. If one allows herself to spend time considering what this transition means to who she is, she will move through it more easily. If she is unaware that it is normal for who she is to shift, she may feel uncomfortable, out of sorts, without knowing why. Acknowledging and working through this identity shift is an important way to listen to and honor our inner bitches who are letting us know through our discomfort that a shift is happening.

Identity continues to develop over our lifetimes. As we develop, as we experience gains and losses, we become different than who we were. Being aware of how we are feeling, what is going on with us at any particular phase of our lives, helps us live our authentic life, the one that our inner bitch is guiding us toward. Every experience we have influences us and adds to who we are. Identity is iterative and incremental.

Intimacy vs Isolation. Erikson believed the young adult years (ages 20-40 years) were a time of intimacy versus isolation – in his view, we found a partner or we felt isolated. As we have already seen, it is not an either/or dichotomy. We all feel isolated at times, even with a partner. And we can find intimacy with more than one person, including friends and family. Nonetheless, young adulthood is often the time we look for and find life partners, as well as close friend groups.

The inner bitch wants to find a partner that allows and encourages her expression. I hear women say over and over that their partners have certain expectations, which have often been built over time, and so the women act in expected ways, without even considering their choice in the situation. I'm talking simple things – meal planning, cooking, shopping, cleaning, laundry, taking the responsibility for family arrangements (carpooling, doctors' appointments, child care, and so on). Women often do many of these things because they think it is expected of them. And it may well be. But – we are often the ones who build the expectations. We play a role in building our own environments. Depending on the stories we have internalized, we may take over these responsibilities because we believe it is what we are supposed to do. We have images in our heads and hearts of what it means to be a married woman, to be a mother, to be a wife. Years and years of indoctrination, media images, and messages have been provided to us. They're not inherently wrong. As long as they fit for each individual. And as long as each individual woman is in tune with her inner bitch and is consciously and intentionally choosing what she wants to do and what works best for her and her own family.

We can experience this tension in our friend groups as well. We develop roles and expectations among our friends, often creating patterns of behavior that stick. We often defer to our friends and their wants because we have done so in the past, and we have been taught through our lives to care for others, be nurturing, put ourselves last. Friendships, often lasting longer than partnered relationships, are critical environments for the growth and expression of our true selves.

We are all developing individuals – each of us individually and as part of a relationship, whether it be a romantic or friend relationship. And as one of us develops, the other is influenced. It is a give and take process, a continual cycle of change. And that can be hard. And it can be beautiful. None of us stays the same. Even if we are not actively growing, we are always changing and shifting. Our views may become more entrenched or flexible; we may become more of what we are. There is no staying the same. Being open to the change, the growth, will allow both individuals to become who they are meant to be – alone and together. Making sure the inner bitch is heard and honored throughout this process will allow you to be true to you. And you will not wake up years later wondering what happened to the you you used to be or wondering who you really are.

Generativity vs Stagnation. Midlife. Feared. Revered. Embraced. We have all heard of people who have dreaded their 40th birthday. The birthday that signifies the ushering in of midlife. And yet, my experience so far has been that midlife is the place to be. Perhaps it is because midlife is the time that I finally began to understand and feel comfortable expressing my inner bitch. How much richer my life would have been, how much less time I would have wasted, had I been in touch with her all along. I certainly had moments of being in touch with her – and I can see her clearly along my life path. But I can also see distinct moments when I buried her or didn't let her express herself. I outright ignored her at some times, even battling with her. As if I knew what I wanted better than my inner bitch.

According to Erikson, midlife (ages 40-65 years) is the time when one explores generativity versus stagnation. What will one leave for upcoming generations? What will our legacy be? How can I contribute so that I make the world a better place? I can mentor, I can teach, I can parent, I can coach, I can build, I can heal, I can paint, I can sculpt, I can compose, I can do so many things that improve my part of the world. And this is generativity.

Stagnation is staying in one spot – not growing, being afraid of change and transition, which is pretty darn silly because change and transition will happen whether or not we want it to. We might as well embrace it. I can see how Erikson's stages have shown up in my life. I am at a point in my life where I am realizing that time is fleeting. Of course we all have that sense – when we go to bed at night as a freshman in college and wake up in the morning as a senior (or so it seems). But when you feel that way as a college senior you still have the sense that life is yet to be lived and there is plenty of time. When you feel that way in your 50s you have a sense of "better get on with what I am really supposed to be doing with my life." And that is motivating and challenging. We no longer have time to waste. And, for those of us who have children, this phase gets easier because another phase has slowly waned. Active parenting can be generativity in its fullest. It can be very difficult to figure out how to make everything happen while you are in the active parenting phase. When children are launched and the house is empty (at least sometimes), the world opens up in a way that it hadn't before.

It becomes harder to ignore the inner bitch. She begins yelling if you don't listen to her. I have been working on listening to her and I hear her more readily. And that is my wish for you as well. That your inner bitch speaks so loudly that you can't ignore her any longer. My hope for those of you who are reading this book at 12, 18, 20, 25, 30, 40, 50+ is that you are tuning into your inner bitch now so that you are rocking it when you are in midlife.

Integrity vs Despair: According to Erikson, the later adult years (ages 65+ years) are a time of reflection and review. We all want to come out on the side of integrity – the feeling that our life was well lived, that we lived our authentic, genuine lives. I don't want to wake up when I am an older adult and think – wow, I actually lived someone else's life. I don't want to feel that I made my decisions for other people, that I behaved in ways I thought other people wanted, that I wasn't aware of what I really wanted. I want to be in my 80's, 90's and hopefully 100's dancing with my inner bitch fully expressing herself. I want to be one with my inner bitch. That is my aspirational picture of integrity.

While we are always in a fluctuating socio-historical context with each generation different from the one before and the one after due to political, societal, financial, and technological influences, it is important to note that I have met older women who feel aimless after their husbands pass away. There is a generational effect here – when these women were young adults, it was less likely that they pursued active careers, so their identities more likely revolved around their relationships. It is important to recognize that times change – and not pass judgment on any generation since each person lives in the context in which they live. It is important to remember that we are both the creators and products of our environment – the social, historical, political, educational environments. And we are influenced by the views of the time. So, women who are in their 70s, 80s and 90s grew up in a different time than I did, and certainly different than my younger readers.

We can learn so many lessons from these wise mavens. The wisdom of older women, as they reflect on their lives, can help us as we reflect on and prepare for ours. They are our spiritual teachers. They can guide us to be the best we can be. And after speaking with many of them, I have learned that I want to be the best me I can be at every age. I don't want to wait for a certain time or age to allow myself to be me. I am me right now. And I am going to let people know me. I don't want to act out of fear of what others think. I don't want to live someone else's story. I want to be conscious and aware of what I think, believe, and do. I want to be thoughtful of what my actions might mean down the road, not just right now. I want my inner bitch to sing and dance and pull out her mighty sparkly wings and fly.

Ending on the side of integrity means we feel good about the decisions we have made and the life we have lived. A sense of despair comes when we are filled with regret about these decisions and our lives. It is normal to feel some regret – all of us wish we had behaved in a different way or taken a detour on our path at some point. But integrating it all into our life story, redeeming those moments, can move us into integrity. I rest easy in this. It can be easy to feel immense pressure to make the right choices, to be accurate in our decision making. Rather, as long as we make the best decision that we can at the time that we make it, then we can rest in the knowledge that every action we take leads us to who we become. Even if we make the "wrong" choice, we can learn from it and move forward. And "wrong" is all perception. Having a rearview mirror perspective offers a biased lens on our lives. We can easily forget the circumstances surrounding our decisions.

Looking behind and looking ahead can give us perspective on the right now. Who we are now is a product of all that came before – the good, the bad, and the ugly. What did we learn from all of it? How did we grow? How can we use all of our myriad experiences to become who we are meant to be? Who we will be later is a product of what we do right now and in the future. Think carefully about what that is. What do you want to be able to say in five, ten, twenty, fifty years? Who do you want to be then? The sooner we are able to connect with our inner bitch and allow her to guide us in our journey, the sooner we will choose to live according to who we really are. You are making decisions now that will influence who you will be later. Rather than letting that terrify you – which would be understandable – let it motivate and excite you.

Pause: Dash

What race are you running? If you are winning, who is losing? Whose treadmill are you on? How much is your time worth? Your precious life energy? When you think about your life span – with birth anchoring one end and death anchoring the other, what does the dash in between symbolize? What provides meaning for you?

Birth Date---Death

While many of us may not relish the idea of sitting alone, thinking about our own death – the other side of the dash – this can be a very empowering exercise. We often sleepwalk through our lives, with one day blurring into the next. Wake up, brush your teeth, get ready for school or work, drive, park, do your thing, walk to your car, drive home, make/eat dinner, spend time with the family, go to bed. Repeat. Repeat. Repeat. Suddenly, years have gone by – filled with subconscious living.

Considering your dash – the beginning and the end of your life bookending what is in between – can be empowering. Take a step back, remember that our continual cycle of repeat is actually our lives. What do you want the dash to mean? How do you want to fill your bookshelf of life? What are the titles of the books – what is the content? Who is the author? What is in your dedication at the front of the book? Who are the people you trust to be the pre-readers of the early drafts?

Imagine your full life – how do you want to fill the middle, between birth and death? Such a small, simple mark of punctuation – and yet, so powerful. What is your dash? How will you live your dash?

Exercise. You will want your journal or a large sheet of paper. This exercise is best done with pen and paper, but an electronic version could work. On one edge of the paper, put your birth date. On the other edge, put a death date. Be very generous with your life – you are embarking on a very healthy journey of discovery, learning self-care, and how to make sure you are the best you can be – so give yourself a long, healthy life. If you do not like the idea of putting a date to the end of your life, which is certainly understandable, put an age – or even "a very long time from now." There is value, though, to recognizing our lives are finite. We do not know what will happen tomorrow. While we all hope our dash is long and that each day is meaningful.

Between those two dates or times, add things you want to make sure you do and experience. Think about how you want to live your life. Consider the following questions.

- What mark do you want to leave on others?
- What would have to change for you to be completely fulfilled?
- What do you want more of on your dash (moments of joy, practicing kindness, time with family)?
- What do you want less of (worry, acting out of fear, overworking)?
- What do you want others to say about you at your celebration of life/funeral?
- What legacy do you want to leave?

******

Understand that our cycle of repeat is our lives, every day. And we are actually living our life now. Not when we finish that degree, or get a new job, or make a certain salary. Now. Today. We are living our dash today. It's a small line – filled with meaning.

Social Prescription

Our social learning results from our individual experiences, the actions/reactions of others, and our environment. Think about how we learn – behaviors are reinforced either directly or indirectly by others. We model our behaviors after people we admire and respect, particularly those with whom we can identify. We learn vicariously by watching how others are reinforced or punished for various behaviors. The people we are with and the environment we are in have strong influences on our resulting behavior. The media has this down – marketing specialists know exactly who should be in a commercial for different shows and viewing times in order to appeal to those viewers.

As we move through our lives, we are continuously learning what is appropriate, acceptable, and admirable. It is how capitalism works. Create a demand for an item by making sure people see those they admire using or wearing it. The craziest styles can turn into fads in this way. Think of the pants that hang around young males' legs rather than their waists. That is not a natural, or comfortable, style. But someone somewhere was wearing his pants that way and it caught on because others wanted to be like him. I occasionally still see this style and want to pull the young man over and tell him that the original wearer has moved on and now wears a belt. But I don't think it would work. The young man has no reason to want to please me – which is the basis of learning theory.

Can you think of any of your own style or behavioral choices that seemed important at the time but upon reflection appear to be fad-following? I remember standing in line with many other parents for Beanie Babies when my children were younger. It seemed very important at the time to get the each new baby as it was released every week (very smart marketing). Those long lines of parents outside the toy store make me think of the long lines outside certain phone stores when a new model is released.

We learn many behaviors and attitudes in this way. It is the primary basis of socialization when children are younger. There are many forces at play when a child is learning how to behave. They want to please their parents for both conscious and subconscious reasons. Consciously, children want to please them because they love their parents and want to see them happy. Children also generally like to follow rules and want to know the parameters in situations. It can be comforting to know the rules or framework of a situation.

According to psychoanalyst Sigmund Freud, a subconscious motivation for good behavior is to avoid the removal of love and care by the parent. When children are little, parents are their key to survival and by learning how to behave they avoid love withdrawal. Children learn quickly that certain behaviors bring reinforcement, which is pleasant and intended to increase the likelihood of that behavior, and other behaviors bring some form of punishment, which is unpleasant and intended to decrease the likelihood of repeat behaviors. Children, then, tend to repeat the reinforced behaviors and decrease the punished behaviors. Reinforcement and punishment can be simple – a quick disapproving parental glance, a verbal "good job."

While parents are trying to get children to behave in certain ways, sometimes there is residual, unintentional learning. Adults hold a lot of power over children, and children know it. Some children rebel in order to assert their own power; others become submissive and defer to that power, sometimes long after that power is effective. This can result in behaviors or childhood stories that we continue to carry with us.

The observable differences between boys and girls are at least partially learned behavior. Little girls are not naturally quiet and demure. We train them to be – we train them to wear pretty little dresses and uncomfortable shoes. We train them to sit quietly and not make too much noise. We buy different toys for boys and girls. We have different expectations for boys and girls. And for men and women.

Little girls begin to model our behavior – as well as what is presented to them in the media, plastered everywhere. There is a science behind advertisements. Messages are not accidental. Women often appear differently than men do in advertisements – with eyes cast down or looking out to the landscape. Men look directly at the camera. The messages given to men and women differ – men are strong, women are gentle, deferring. Subtle and not so subtle messages are bombarding little girls all the time – of course, they are bombarding women as well, reinforcing the societal messages of flawless women in unrealistic shoes. Little girls are even more susceptible, seeking role models as they are developmentally trying to figure out how they fit into the world, what role they are supposed to play, how they are supposed to act. Do we want them to learn these hidden messages or do we want to stand up and teach them to not bury their little inner bitches, to keep them in full view, and stand up for themselves in a strong, assertive, acceptable way?

Girls are reinforced for behaving in ways that are socially prescribed. They learn certain behaviors are "better" than others. And the feedback loop continues uninterrupted unless something interferes. And equally dangerous is that little boys are also seeing these advertisements, getting these messages, and building their expectations of what the world looks like through their absorption of the implicit, and sometimes explicit, bias presented in the media. We are sold a bill of goods and can find ourselves disappointed when life does not turn out the way we have been led to believe.

Social media has a similar influence on our learning. We repeatedly see people living fun, glamorous lives, with pictures rosy and beautiful. We don't see the arguments or the lost keys or the wrong turns that led to that beautiful picture. And we are trained to measure ourselves against what we see. Our lives don't look like that.

These messages are passed around freely – be like this, wear this, drive this, do this. And they are not inherently wrong or harmful. But we often unquestioningly accept that these messages are what we should aspire to or want. This goes back to Maslow's hierarchy of needs. Which need are we trying to meet if we are wearing our jeans around our knees or stilettos on our feet? Probably not basic clothing which is intended to shelter our bodies. We are looking to fill our belonging and esteem needs. Why are we majoring in biology when our true love is art history? We are likely trying to fill our esteem needs, but we will find that trying to fill our esteem needs without consulting our inner bitch will prevent us from moving to self-actualizing. We can be respected and admired for what we do, even if we are doing it for the wrong reasons. We have been reinforced when we tell others we want to major in biology, or we want to become a doctor. "Wow." "That's impressive." "You must be really smart." Those messages are hard to ignore – we like to be reinforced. And if we are reinforced often enough we may even begin to believe what we are saying. Our inner bitch may be telling us otherwise. But we may quiet her because, on the surface, it seems more important to gain respect from others than authenticity from ourselves.

When one becomes more in tune with her inner bitch, she begins to understand that many of these behaviors and thoughts have been learned over time, and consequently can be unlearned. Sounds simple, but it is not easy. Retraining our minds to reframe our thoughts takes work, but it is so worth it. Beginning to understand what you really want rather than what will make others like you is a step in the direction of living your abundant life. And most of the time, other people don't care what you major in, what kind of car you drive or the brand of shoes you wear. They may have a moment of being impressed, but that often passes. If your friends continue to judge you on the basis of these things, you may want to consider reframing your friend group.

Pause: Beauty of Mistakes

We have been taught to feel shame about our mistakes, to hide them from others, and to punish ourselves repeatedly for them. Shifting this belief and reclaiming mistakes will help us reclaim our inner bitch. Mistakes are an important part of the learning process; they help us learn what works and what doesn't. Normalizing mistakes, making them an accepted and celebrated part of our society, will reduce the negative, debilitating emotion of shame we feel when we make mistakes. We want to begin to see their beauty, their importance. We become better through our mistakes. We become who we are. We become beautiful.

Well into my adulthood, I was afraid of making mistakes. I was afraid of letting people down. I was afraid of not being good enough. Well, actually I wasn't afraid of that – I **knew** I wasn't good enough. I was afraid that I would **never** be good enough. I wanted to believe that someday I would be "enough." I would have accomplished "enough." I would have "enough" education. I would have "enough" experience. Then I would be okay. Then I would be worthy. But that day never came. Like the Lifecycle at the gym – the steps kept coming while I was not going anywhere. I stayed in the same place, but kept climbing the steps, out of breath, muscles aching, sweat dripping, heart racing. I finally began to understand that the acceptance needed to come from within myself. And that could only be accomplished if my inner bitch was allowed to express herself, if she was allowed to come out of hiding, if she could begin to peer out from behind the crap among which she was hidden.

There were moments along the way that I had glimpses of my inner bitch. I made a big step in excavating her when I realized I didn't want to become a doctor. That was a long road for me, as I think it is for others. I have witnessed many a college student who thinks he/she is going to become a doctor – for so many reasons. For me, it was multi-faceted. First, I wanted to make my dad proud. And I couldn't figure out how to do that. I kept living up to expectations, but I couldn't possibly exceed them. "We expect nothing less." The best and better is all that was good enough.

Second, it was rewarding to tell people that I wanted to become a doctor. They were so impressed and thought that I was amazing. The external positive reinforcement can easily keep people on that path long after they should step off. I was smart. I was hardworking. I would have made a great doctor. But I realized I wanted more from my life than being a doctor. I didn't want to be a doctor. I just wanted to be "good enough." I began to have a bit of insight during my early twenties that I could be "good enough" doing something I liked. I was beginning to release the pressure valve, albeit slowly.

While this sounds self-deprecating, it wasn't. For so many years, I was working towards being good enough, valued, validated. I was looking externally, trying to meet and exceed expectations that were "nothing less than," "only the best," "of course you achieved that." I consider it a great accomplishment and amazing insight to understand I could be "good enough" in the way of "good enough is good enough" kind of way. When I began to realize I didn't need to be perfect, just good enough, I began to feel hope and optimism. I could be me, the real me, not the me that I believed others expected – the one that achieved 'nothing less' 'only the best'. That pressure was too great. Those expectations were unattainable. I began to want to be good enough. And when I began to have that as a goal, I began to thrive. Thrive as me. Me who is good enough as I am. Me who is worthy because I am. I often viewed those three years of pre-med as a mistake. But that 'mistake' led me to the path of understanding what I wanted and what I didn't want. I have numerous examples in my personal and professional life of what appeared to be a mistake but instead was an important learning opportunity.

We often feel that making a mistake makes us less of a person, shows we really are incompetent, stupid, unworthy, you name it. We go down a negative spiral, adding meaning to the mistake beyond the circumstances. Yet, every mistake is an opportunity someone took. A risk taken. Those are good things. Fear of making mistakes is usually more harmful than the actual mistake.

Exercise. We are often encouraged to minimize or hide our mistakes. Yet, mistakes and failure are stepping stones to success. We learn much less from the times we are successful on our first try. We iterate and improve every time things go other than we planned. Sharing our mistakes and failures would normalize them, help us learn from others, and improve our collective mental health. We can work on dismantling these cultural messages and stories as we find our inner bitches and let them express themselves.

Spend some time and make a list of at least 5 things you consider to be mistakes in your life. They do not have to be big mistakes; they can be small, seemingly inconsequential mistakes. If you are thinking of them, they are meaningful to you. After you have done that, write down next to each mistake what you have learned from it and how it helped you become who you are today. Even if a mistake was truly a bad choice, it contributed to who you are today.

Then, as you go about your daily life and you feel like you made a mistake, ask yourself a few questions.

- Did you make the best decision you could with the information you had at that time?
- Were you thoughtful about what you were doing?
- Would you make the same decision now if you only had the same information?
- What did you learn from making that decision that you wouldn't have learned had you not made that decision?
- How have you moved forward by making that mistake?

Embrace each mistake as a stepping stone on the path to becoming who you are.

Societal Influences on the Inner Bitch

I've witnessed and experienced that societal messages (judgments) are often delivered by other girls or women. The social environment is rife with women of all ages judging each other. Does bringing someone down elevate you? No, but many do it because subconsciously they believe it will. That is zero sum game thinking. A zero sum game is when one person's gain is directly balanced by someone else's loss. Everything equals zero at the end of the game. But life is not a zero sum game. We all have gifts and talents, and we are all beautiful. You can be beautiful, and I can be beautiful. Some may say we are fighting for the same resources, but I don't think so. It reminds me of the beer dives we used to have at the pool. Cases of beer were thrown into the deep end and dozens of adult would jump in and grab beer as quickly as they could. I must say, I was pretty good at beer dives. And my husband Brian and I would tag team it as well – he would go in the water and toss the beer to me so he could have free hands to keep grabbing beer. More and more beer. So here's the ridiculous part. Neither one of us even drink beer. And this was at a private pool, so everyone there could afford to buy beer. But when there is a perceived shortage, the competition can get fierce. The scarcity mentality is an incredibly powerful motivator for thoughts and behavior.

I see perception of scarcity on college campuses; there are only a few good partners, a few A's given, a few good jobs to get. There is a feeling that there is not enough for everyone. And so the judgments are wicked. And particularly around eating and body size. Over my 25 years teaching at a higher education institution, the issues have remained the same. The concerns have remained consistent – self-doubt, self-deprecation, fear of judgment from others, actual judgment from others, body dysphoria, the desire for effortless perfection. We have not come a long way, baby[7]. We are in the same place we have always been. And we will stay there until we learn to let our inner bitches express themselves more.

The media

Photoshopping is a curse of the modern world. Young girls may not be aware that all the pictures they see are photoshopped. Older women see beautiful women with no wrinkles, no cellulite, no sagging skin. So is built expectation and the norm of beauty. But it is mostly unattainable. A few select women have "the look" that works for modeling. And then editing does the rest.

Social media also contributes. People generally don't put their humiliating experiences on social media. Like the time they left the bathroom with toilet paper tucked into their dress. Or the time they locked their keys in the car, which was filled with groceries, ice cream melting as they stood helplessly outside looking in. Instead the posts are about beautiful experiences which happen on sunny, not humid days, with gorgeous friends, and a dog with a bow around its neck. A steady diet of this can make anyone believe that the world is full of perfect people who have it all together.

And that's all just about looks and appearances– the expectations set in these media sources also involve the so-called duties of each gender – the cooking (women) or the grilling (men). The subtle (and not so subtle) indoctrination and socialization of these rules into our minds – without even thinking about it because it is below our consciousness – affect our inner bitch. We want to be able to express ourselves in the way we want to and do the things we like, whether it is considered gender-appropriate or not. Allowing your inner bitch to break out of those gender norms is healthy and allows full expression of you as an individual. And it will help break the molds that keep other women from expressing their full selves. Can you imagine what our country would look like if half our adult population was fully engaged, whole women who are in touch with their inner bitches? Complete, unadulterated bad-assery. The ripple effects would be tremendous.

Ripple effects of unadulterated bad-assery

Let's imagine briefly. Knowing where to start is difficult because the effects would spread across the lifespan. Let's start with the young woman who has just finished high school. She will know if she wants to go to college to study a field of her choice, one which she will completely rock because she loves the area and knows it is a good fit. Or she will decide that college is not for her right now, and she will enter the workforce as the power that she is, finding a job at which she can thrive and excel. Or she will travel and gain experience in cultures and worlds different from her own.

When and if she decides to find a partner, she will know herself before she walks into a partnership. She will not lose her identity in this partnership. Instead she will be complemented by her partner, enabling her true self to grow and shine. She will continue to pursue her life's work if she decides that this path is right for her and her partner. Every step will be taken after consideration of what is right for her, her inner bitch, and those around her.

Finding and expressing your inner bitch does not mean decisions are selfish, with consideration only of one's self. Rather it means considering what one wants, what would be best for you, and what is best for others. After careful contemplation a decision can be made that allows everyone to be as whole as possible. The decision may involve making a choice that is not one you would have made had you been alone. But if you are not alone, these choices are worth it, as long as they are made thoughtfully and consciously.

As the empowered woman and her inner bitch move through adulthood, she knows that failure is an important part of life and that most successes stem from one or more failures. She does not hide her mistakes. She is willing to share them and talk about why they are important to her, demystifying perfection. If we don't share our mistakes, our failures, our missteps, women believe that everything is easy for everyone else, but not for ourselves.

The empowered woman will decide what clothes and shoes she wears and why, and she will teach young girls to do the same. Clothes that restrict ease of movement, shoes that make walking difficult, clothes that make playing on the jungle gym challenging – these will be thought about before wearing. If she truly likes those shoes or those clothes, then she will wear them! But if she doesn't like the way she feels when or after wearing them (restrictive pantyhose, sore feet from high heels), she will consider when and if she must wear them. She will wear clothes that express her personality and creativity and also allow her to dance and turn a cartwheel if she so desires.

She will be willing to talk about money, to make her own financial decisions, to stand up for herself if she thinks someone might be taking advantage of her. She will have her own financial plan and goals. And she will be willing to claim that she wants more of it. She wants financial security and financial abundance.

The complete unadulterated badass brings to the workplace management skills that encourage people to express their ideas, take calculated risks, and grow in their careers. She has no need to hold people back or feel threatened by their successes. Her team's successes reflect on her and she is able to redirect the shine back onto them. And through it all, people will be fulfilled, merging their lives and their careers in a way that is congruent with their values and their dreams. It is an awesome image – to have unabashed empowerment, real skill expression, authentic and genuine conversation and idea exchange – in the work place. The power that could be unleashed is unimaginable. Every level and type of job could be impacted – because our inner bitches have encouraged us to speak up for ourselves and others in a way that is clear and not bitchy so we can have our voices heard and others are able to listen.

This describes the workplace manager inner bitch. We can also imagine the nurse inner bitch – who is willing to speak up for the patient to any one in a white coat. Research has demonstrated that nurses hold much power to ensure the safety of patients, and yet this is not always leveraged due to the intimidation by doctors, both male and female. The nurse inner bitch will advocate for herself and the patient, making the workplace what she wants it to be.

The doctor inner bitch will be willing to listen to others, accept her limitations, and intentionally decrease the white coat syndrome and work diligently to increase health equity. The lawyer inner bitch will be willing to speak her truth and stand firm in her own power.

The teacher inner bitch will be willing to nurture students beyond the mandatory testing ubiquitous in the school system. She will allow student inner bitches to express themselves and create an egalitarian learning environment free from gender stereotypes for both boys and girls. And she will be willing to grade papers with a lens of what is right for the student, not of creating mini-models of herself.

We can imagine the ripple effects of all kinds of working inner bitches. Each of these professional inner bitches will be working toward work-life integration, participating in meaningful and important work while enjoying their full lives outside of work.

When and if a woman becomes a parent, this full-blown inner bitch bad-assery will compound itself dramatically. Decisions regarding who will stay home with the child or if both parents will work will be made jointly, with consideration of all involved. The fascinating part of all of this is that the woman will know what she wants. How crazy is that! It is my belief that most partners have wanted the woman to do what would allow herself full expression, but that we as women didn't always know what that was because our inner bitches were so hidden and silenced. Better decisions will be made. Parenting will focus on each person's strength rather than gender roles and norms. No longer will the parent need the child to fulfill her own unmet desires as an expression of the parent's worth. Children will be allowed to express their own selves in a way that does not reflect the worth of a parent because the woman will know her worth on her own.

Emotions will not be suppressed and instead will be managed in a healthy manner. Toys will be appropriate for both genders, so talents and strengths can be nurtured without consideration of gender expectations. Little girls will not silence themselves as they grow into their adolescent years, but instead will become powerful sources of great ideas and energy. They will not succumb to the false ideals fed to them by media or by the effortless perfection portrayed by social media. They will feel good about themselves inherently because they know who they are and that they are worthy just because. And then they will finish high school knowing what they want to do next because they have been asking themselves who they are as individuals rather than who they are in relation to everyone else.

And best of all, this is not all about gains for women. We all win. Males and females alike. This sounds like it could be a nightmare for men, but it's truly not. Having a woman know who she is, without having her true self suffocated under societal expectations, personal fears of rejection, years of messaging, can only be a good thing. Relationships will be more genuine. Communication will be more open. Utopia? Probably not. But I believe we would unleash an incredible power that women are not even aware they have. The power for good. The power for self. The power of expression. The power of the inner bitch.

Dimming the Inner Bitch

My story happened within the context of my family. And my culture and my society. When we look at the systems within which we live, we can see the multi-layered effect of the messages we are provided. Media delivers our societal messages of how we are supposed to look, what we are supposed to wear, what we need to own in order to fit in and excel.

Our education system is a great vector of socialization. This is where we learn to sit quietly, follow the rules, stand in line, and wait our turn. It's where we learn to not be too noisy on the playground, and to talk only after we've raised our hands and been called on. Our neighborhoods are the agents and monitors of social rules and hierarchies – whose yard is the best to play in, what happens when we are different in some way, how should we dress, what video games should we be playing.

Our families are the microcosms of all that is external while also trying to be the purveyor of the internal. It is a challenging task. And parents are people too. Parents come with multiple roles, multiple hats that they wear. I may be idealizing the past, but it seems like the outside context used to be more of an ally to the family. The neighborhood was a partner in raising children, providing many parental eyes on them, nudging the children toward prosocial behavior. When the media was less powerful. But regardless, we live in the world as it is now. We can all encourage our children to be good people while allowing them to be seen and their voices to be heard.

Silencing is a phenomenon that often happens in early adolescent females, but which has underpinnings long before. Adolescent females begin to quiet themselves around others, putting others' needs and desires before their own. I believe, for myself, it happened before adolescence. Perhaps the symptoms became more evident at that time, but I learned to silence myself much earlier. I learned how to fly under the radar, so as not to attract attention. In parallel, I learned that putting my head down, learning and achieving, brought me positive accolades. I became the smart one, the reliable one, the responsible one. And yet, at the same time, accomplishments were met with the reaction of increasing expectations. "We expect nothing less." "We expect success and excellence." It is what I began to expect of myself as well. But the damage was being done, every single time. No need to celebrate – I only did what was expected. Each time. The innate desire to be validated, to be praised, to be appreciated was left unmet. Each accomplishment was put aside in favor of the new and better next one. It's little wonder that, over four decades later, I am still trying to achieve and surpass internal expectations.

And we dim the inner bitch, right at the moment she could be shining with accomplishment. We don't take the time to celebrate but quickly move on to the next goal. Awareness of the dimming and the silencing can enable us to take steps toward letting our inner bitch express and celebrate herself. And you!

Pause: Whose Life am I Living?

Whose life do you want to live? Why? Do you know what others think or do you live your life based on what you are guessing they are thinking? Or based on past or current expectations.

Expectations can be dangerous. When one is successful, one is expected to succeed. It becomes common place and routine. And the hamster wheel continues to turn. Getting off that success cycle can be extremely difficult. How does one measure success if one is always expected to succeed? What if one gets tired and needs a rest? What if one wants to sit out a round?

Setting high expectations is important. We rise to expectations. We understand how to measure ourselves against expectations – and when those expectations are not met, we know what the gap is. The problem lies in the individuals who set extremely high personal expectations, accept nothing less, and ultimately value the achievement of those expectations much less than they value the striving toward that expectation. Those who believe that we will be worthy when we achieve X. People like me. There are lots of us out there. And often we are female. We internalize the expectations and we internalize the expectation to meet the expectations.

Parental expectations are especially powerful. They often outlive their usefulness – or even their truth. Sometimes expectations shared when children are young are cemented in the young child's mind and are not adapted as the child and the parents grow. Parents sometimes don't even know what they have instilled in their children from an early age.

Parents may express things when children are younger, typically idealistic statements and expectations, which parents often adapt in their own heads and hearts over time as they watch the child grow. However, when the child is young, parents' words, views, declarations are everything to the child. It is truth.

Even if it is not. This includes any misaligned, negative statement about worth, ability, tendency, character. The words become prophesy, a beacon for children, while in a parent's mind it might only have been a statement which resulted from a bad day at work. The power of words spoken from the source of all that is needed as a child cannot be overstated. Parents must be hyper-vigilant regarding the statements they offer their children. Parental expectations may shift and strengthen as parents see the abilities develop in their children.

But a few things can happen:

1. Parents continue to have exceedingly high expectations for children's success and accomplishments because it is all they know, and/or they are guided by the individualistic, materialistic, hedonistic, achievement-oriented messages of our culture.

2. Parents develop more realistic expectations as their children become their own selves, but they fail to explicitly update their expectation statement to their children.

3. Parents update their expectations but the power of the early message is seared into the child's brain and outweighs the recent messaging.

Exercise. How do past or present parental expectations play a role in your actions/behaviors/decisions? Can you see patterns that demonstrate the power of parental expectations?

Mind map or journal messages that have guided your behavior. What are your internalized parental expectations? Are they still relevant?

Take a good look at your parents. Your mind's eye can be very powerful. Take off the historical lens and see who they are now. If you have the opportunity, ask them what they want for you. Ask them what makes them happy. You may hear similar expectations from what you have internalized; you may not.

At some point, you have to live your own life – not theirs. Think about what this means to you and whether you need to reframe your thoughts and ultimately your life.

Childhood Stories

Do you remember societal/parental messages about "reality"? How things "were"? In our early childhood, we have a very limited view of what life is like – and it is created by watching our parents and sometimes other adults. They color our view, offering their lens with which we see everything and it can be difficult for us to later remove the lens. We may not even know we are wearing outdated lenses. In childhood, we relied on our parents for survival. We quickly adapted to their wishes because they were the primary force in our lives. We didn't have a broader perspective of what the world was like outside of our small microcosm. And so we internalized the views of our family, our neighborhood, our community, our teachers. Often without question. Until later, when our cognitive abilities and our exposure to external environments coalesced. But it is much harder to counteract these messages after they are ingrained, even when we are cognitively more mature. These messages, these stories have become embedded in our minds and hearts because they have emotional meaning. We believe them to be truth, and we often don't question them. We have no reason to question them. Until we do.

When we were children, we were susceptible to messages that were intentionally and unintentionally delivered to us. Our parents, our teachers, toys, advertisements – all worked together to socialize us. That is, in fact, one of the implicit tasks of our community. We learn to be good citizens, to fit into our society. We learn to stand in line, follow the rules, pay attention to people in authority, be attuned to reinforcement or dissuasion. Our survival depends on this. Until it doesn't.

We internalize the messages we receive when we are young. Many times these messages were unintentionally delivered or reinforced. And we are often the unwilling, even unaware, vector of the message. For example, I learned very early that being busy was admirable, a good thing, impressive. Couple that with my tendency toward responsibility and achievement, and I believed that my worth was dependent on my productivity, my accomplishment. Our society also reinforces that message incessantly. "Keeping busy?" is a common greeting. As if that is more important than "how are you?" Not that we really mean it when we ask that either, but that is a different book.

We need to explore our internalized messages so we can understand what we believe and why. As children, we are taught to behave in ways that essentially ensure our social survival – to act as good citizens, family members, part of the society in which we live. This socialization is important, but it can also lead to a long-term internalization of beliefs that no longer serve us. Examining those messages that essentially flow through us is an important part of uncovering what we really believe and why. Some of our internalized messages are valuable and we may decide to keep them. Others may need to be updated. And still others may need to be asked politely to leave. But first we need to figure out what they are.

Do you remember societal/parental messages about reality? Did your parents offer views that appeared to be statements of truth, but were really reflections of their own values, beliefs, perceptions or possibly even internalized messages from their own parents?

I internalized who I was as a child, and those messages were reinforced consistently. My value and worth was gained from being busy, accomplishing, looking a certain way, following the societal doctrine of beauty and being. And I carried that story with me for a very long time. Everything I did was based on that story. Every situation was seen through that lens. I strove for acknowledgment and validation. My childhood story was that "we expect nothing less." That fit perfectly with my beliefs about myself. So I wore that cloak of never being able to exceed expectations for most of my life, without even really knowing whose expectations I was trying to exceed. Everyone's, really. I tried to exceed everyone's expectations, usually created in my own head. A difficult task, for sure.

This story played out in many different ways, with various outcomes. On the positive side, this story led to my academic success, going to graduate school without going into debt, etc. Externally, all good outcomes. Internally, I could not achieve enough. I felt like I always needed to step it up, do more, and hit the next level.

There are many stories that we collectively carry with us, knowingly or unknowingly. For example, we should want more and more – whether it be possessions, degrees, titles, or achievements. We should use our time productively, with "productive" meaning we have a deliverable. We should sleep as little as possible, because less sleep is a sign of commitment and importance. Being thin means we are happy. As if somehow our body size and type controls our emotions, and thinness means all other things are achieved as well.

What stories have been incubating within you? Were you praised for certain behaviors? Like being good, quiet, industrious, generous, and passive? I learned very quickly that being busy meant being valuable and important. I lost myself through academics. Undoubtedly better than drugs and alcohol, but with ramifications nonetheless. Extracting myself from the achievement orientation has been difficult – I have been too willing to work too hard, too much, burying my true desires and self behind the needs of others at the workplace, whether it be emotional chaos from team members or deadlines (real or manufactured). I became the rescuer, the one who would be loyal to the end. After a while, though, this self-sacrifice took a toll on my health and well-being.

Finding the stories that dwell within us is simple, but not easy. Your constant companion, your noisy roommate, is very quick to remind you of how you are "supposed" to be, of when you are not following the rules and conforming to the person others expect you to be. Or at least how you think others expect you to be. The irony of all of this is that we often carry these stories with us when no one else really cares. Others are not thinking about us the way we think they are.

We often bring the childhood stories we internalized into adulthood. Sometimes we learn stories in adulthood and generalize them into other situations. Our society encourages us to believe the stories that we are being told, whether individually or collectively. I have heard many say that they began to fear that they would be failures in everything they do because they failed at one thing. The story that mistakes are bad or undesirable is one that our society perpetuates.

What gender stories were there in your childhood that might have encouraged your inner bitch to go in hiding?

Girls are quiet, girls help out, girls defer to others first, girls allow others to go first. This is not our parents' fault. As a society we have indoctrinated children in similar ways.

Individually, we need to recognize our stories and begin to rewrite them. This can take some time as we increase our awareness of why we do what we do, what messages our noisy roommate is giving us, and how we see the world. The first step to rewriting our stories is awareness. Journaling and mind mapping can be instrumental in this awareness. Spending time listening to your inner bitch, paying attention to what comes up when journaling, can bring these stories to light. Being aware of your own reactions and thoughts as you go about your day can increase awareness. When does your heart begin to race a little? When do you begin to feel the pit in your stomach? Or the cold, clammy feeling of shame? By catching those feelings at the beginning, you can often identify the cause. When you have identified potential triggers, think about the situation. Is this real? Are you reacting to something from your past or are you truly reacting to the facts of the situation right now?

I have spent many hours over my lifetime worrying what others thought of me, assuming they must be disappointed in or unhappy with me. When I looked at the facts – I haven't received an email from someone for a few days or a text response within an hour – I realized that there are likely many explanations beyond my own behind the reason for a lack of an email or text response. In fact, I began to realize that people actually think about me much less often than I attributed to them. They weren't thinking less of me – they were simply thinking about me less.

That is a good thing. My noisy roommate was telling me that others were judging me and withholding communication because they were so disgusted with me. My inner bitch told me they were incredibly busy doing the things they were doing, not paying attention to me. And that if they were unhappy with me, they would let me know.

The moment I decided to wait until someone expressed dissatisfaction to me rather than preemptively assuming dissatisfaction was the moment I began rewriting my story. I spent so much energy proactively assuming the worst, working at making things better when things were fine to begin with. That energy was available for other, more valuable endeavors when I began rewriting that ending. Prior to this, I would actually make things worse by pointing out things I had done that I wasn't proud of, apologizing for things I was actually not even responsible for, all of which had me highlighting my negative energy. Since releasing all of this, and rewriting my story, I have been able to approach conversations more positively rather than constantly waiting for the other shoe to drop. What we focus on grows. And by pointing out things I was sorry for, I was making that grow in others' minds.

There are financial stories, career stories, family stories, religion stories, and so on. When someone is having a hard time saving money, examining the stories her parents had about money can be helpful. Every adult is making decisions based on the lessons they bring from their own experiences. For example, if they were brought up during times of economic hardship, their decisions regarding purchases will be colored by that – sometimes in divergent ways. One parent might decide their children will not experience deprivation and lean toward excessive purchase, while another parent might instill frugality as a value.

These kinds of money stories can have an enormous impact on how you feel about money. The same thing can happen with how you view your career or work ethic, what your parenting beliefs are, or whether you feel it is okay to explore other religions. Parents, teachers, society all work hard to socialize us – believing they are doing the right thing. And often they are doing good things. It is how we interpret those messages and how much we internalize them that can lead to challenges.

If we operate from beliefs that we don't know we have, then there is likely a hidden story somewhere within. It is worth identifying those stories to see if they still fit. Sometimes our stories are things we choose to keep. Other times, though, it is an eye-opening experience to see why we behave or believe the way we do. Stop living according to other people's stories. Become the author of your own story, and let you inner bitch be the main character. That is the only way to live your own life.

Pause: Understanding Your Story

What story are you living out? What are you doing to contribute to your current life? How are you creating your own experience?

Spend some time on this exercise. Come back to it occasionally as you may find that once you begin to find your stories, you are able to identify them more readily. Making note of your stories will help you know to pause and think about your behavior and decisions, deciding whether you are acting from the place of a story or from your true desires.

How to find the stories you carry with you:

The way you talk about yourself and your life – your **story** – has a great deal to do with what shows up in your day-to-day experience. Your thoughts create filters through which you view your life. About 80% of your experience is perception; about 20% is fact. Your thoughts, your story exert a powerful influence over your life. You are the hero of your own story.

Consider the following questions, and reflect on the stories of your life. These stories can be carried over from the internalized messages from the previous exercise. They might be something we interpreted and implemented in our lives, without hearing explicit messages about them. Give yourself the gift of time for this exercise, as it is fundamental to finding and excavating your inner bitch and allowing her to guide you.

This exercise is part of the excavation. And excavation can take time. Allow yourself to return to this exercise as desired or needed. Journal or mind map your responses to the following question.

Part one is about who you are and the stories which may be core to how you see yourself and consequently motivate your thoughts and behavior. Part two is about specific areas in your life in which you might have stories. I recommend doing both parts – and revisiting them often as you begin to become more aware of your stories. Excavating is accomplished in layers; finding one story will often lead to the awareness of others.

Exercise, Part One

o   What stories were passed on to you by others?
o   What stories did you create based on your observations?
o   What stories do you tell yourself?
o   What stories does society/our culture tell us?
o   Do you still carry them with you?
o   Do they still fit?
o   How does this story drive your behavior?
o   Whose story are you living?

I recommend that you listen to the song "Unwritten," by Natasha Bedingfield, after you have finished this part of the exercise. I listen to this song several times a week because it inspires me to be the hero of my own story, with the pen in my own hand.

Then consider the following questions.

o   What would happen if you rewrote some of the stories?
o   Which would you rewrite?
o   Which would you develop more fully?
o   How can you begin to rewrite your story?
o   What can you do today to begin the editing and rewriting?

Exercise, Part Two

We have stories about all areas of our lives: finances, career/work, family, religion, free time. How was money treated in your family? How much is enough? Where does your work ethic come from? What role does your family play in your decision-making? What stories are you carrying about religion? Where does spirituality come in? And free time – wow. Free time is considered dangerous by some – it's an opportunity for you to get into trouble. Stay busy so you are safe. What about the oh-so-familiar phrase 'wasting time'?

o   Money
o   Career
o   Work
o   Free time
o   Relationships
o   Family
o   Gender
o   Your body/health/weight
o   Religion
o   Others?

Choose an area of your life to examine the stories you may be living out. Consider the following questions:

o   What stories were passed on to you by others?
o   What stories did you create based on your observations?
o   What stories do you tell yourself about this area?
o   What stories does society/our culture tell us?
o   Do you still carry them with you?
o   Do they still fit?
o   How does this story drive your behavior?
o   Whose story are you living?

Then consider the following questions.

o   What would happen if you rewrote some of your stories?
o   Which would you rewrite?
o   Which would you develop more fully?
o   How can you begin to rewrite your story?
o   What can you do today to begin the editing and rewriting?

Chapter 3: The Paradox of Success

I grew up in a safe environment where I was well-loved. The hard part about telling our stories is that we often feel like we are going to hurt someone else in doing it. There are other characters in the plot, and those characters can only be portrayed the way the author perceives them. So it is in my story. I can only portray historical events as I saw them, through my own lens. That does not mean it is "reality" – most reality is perception. We all observe our lives with a lens, which colors our perception of events, meaning, intention. That perception colors our feelings and subsequent actions. And that is important. When we consciously and purposefully work on changing that story, that perception, when we take off that lens and try on a different lens, just like in the optical store, we can see things differently. We can change how we look back, and more important, how we move forward. If we can change our lens, we can change our feelings, our thoughts, our actions, our habits, our lives.

All this to say – this story is mine. And it has much less to do with what actually happened then it does with what my child-self perceived and internalized. And I brought my self to the event, to the story in all things. My personality, my tendencies, my experiences, my filters – all play a role in the meaning attributed to events.

I want to note that in the telling of my story, I am thoughtful about the others in my story. Because finding, releasing, and embracing my inner bitch does not mean becoming thoughtless about others or becoming bitchy in our interactions. Rather it means making sure that our truth, our thoughts, our 'me-ness' is expressed in a thoughtful, healthy way which allows our 'me-ness' to be heard and validated – even if that happens just by ourselves, for ourselves.

I'm so busy

One of my earliest memories is putting on a play for my mom when I was about 4. I was at an ironing board, pretending to iron, while running to and fro doing a million other things at the same time – demonstrating my worth through my busyness. I was so proud of doing all those things at one time. I was so busy! I was important! I do not recall my mom's reaction, but knowing my sweet mom, I can imagine it was pleasure and reinforcing – not because of the busyness, which likely meant nothing to her. Rather, it was the drama and excitement I was exhibiting to which she was reacting. She was proud of my creativity. But I internalized a different message – being busy means being worthy.

If my mom reacted positively, and I'm certain she would have because that is the kind of person she is, I interpreted the positive reinforcement for my busyness, likely in combination with my great acting prowess. I was then repeatedly reinforced for being busy, for doing multiple things at one time – for achieving. One could think of it a bit like a virus, which spreads and spreads. Or, I could reframe it and think of it as a beautiful bold thread that provides contrast, color, and expression to my life tapestry, vibrantly connecting all things.

I have spent my life being busy – although over time the busyness has shifted. I almost always have multiple irons in the fire, none of which I am willing to drop without a fight (typically internal). Why is it that I am compelled to do all these things? Some of it is because I just like to learn. I like to be planning things (sort of – I also hate planning things). I like to make things happen. My career has revolved around this skill and affinity. But if I'm really honest with myself, there is more to it than that. There is safety in having multiple opportunities going on at the same time. If I fail at one, I can move to another. The importance of safety throughout my life has been prominently displayed, mostly evident through hindsight. Having a back-up plan meets my security needs, like having a spare tire in my car.

Being busy was also safe in two other ways. If I was busy, others left me alone so I was able to buffer myself with busyness. And being busy meant I didn't have the time or space to experience my unhappiness. Busyness was a bit like a heavy parka, cloaking me in protection but also not letting anyone, including myself, see what was inside.

The busyness is also about achievement. The road to achievement is paved with multiple tasks. Busyness plus achievement are strong threads in my life.

A coaching client said to me that he hates to lose more than he likes to win. I get that. We often don't remember our wins as clearly as we remember our losses. And for achievers like me, the wins, the achievements, well, they just end up in a meaningless pile after a while. Not that I get so many that I lose track – it is not that at all. It is that we don't appreciate and celebrate each one fully. Each is only a marker on the road to something else, a step on the way to more. A new goal, a new achievement. Taking the time to celebrate each success, each accomplishment, would be an important step. But those achievements are the ladder on which we are trying to reach – not success – worthiness. And the ladder resembles the machine in the gym, where the steps just keep coming, one right after the other, with the stepper never going anywhere different.

And yet, our failures? They stand out for us – highlighted in our history. Moments of shame, proof of our ineptness and our lack of worth. Ridiculous, isn't it? When I think about how much energy and time I have spent ruminating over something that didn't go right, I am saddened for my inner bitch, who just kept getting buried with more and more crap. What could I have done? I could have addressed the issue – and figured out what I have learned from that "failure" or that miss. Usually it meant nothing, truly. It was a blip on the screen of life that others didn't think anything of and certainly don't remember, don't attribute such negative meaning, in the way that I do. Instead, I could learn to address the lack of success for what it is and move on to other things – realizing that my future successes are usually the result of my past and current failures. Through not accomplishing something I learn how I can accomplish it the next time. If you have the opportunity, watch a baby learn to walk. They do not fall on the ground and lament about what a loser they are because they can't walk on their first try. They get up and try again. Again and again. Often with applause from those around.

I'm not talking about big things here – I'm talking about the self-perceived silly remark made in a meeting, the time I stumbled over my words in front of my boss, or when I didn't speak up with my brilliant thought when I wish I had. Or when I lost my temper with my children or spouse. Over and over and over again.

It's interesting how the achievements tend to be external – things – and the failures are internal – how I behaved or didn't behave. The external achievements are trivial in my life story. The internal failures – paramount. If I were to shift my focus to my internal achievements – well, those are amazing.

Celebrating the *internal* achievements is one way to release the inner bitch from her internal shackles. Those kids we raised – they are AWESOME. I've learned to take a moment to feel the warm glow when they open the door for others, when they speak to someone who looks emotionally down, when they send a text expressing their love and gratitude toward me, when they feel the pain of others because their empathy muscle is strong. I did so many more things right than I did wrong in the raising of our kids. And yet – what do I find myself spiraling around? The times I wish I had acted differently. This is when changing my lens, shifting my focus, is so critical. Celebrating our children – who they have become – allows them and me to shine. Bask in that light – which will change my emotions, which will change my thoughts, which will change my behaviors, which will change my habits, which will change my life. Focusing on what I didn't do right or what I might have done wrong (because they can be different) puts me in a mindset of lack, rather than abundance. My mistakes have allowed our children to learn. And to realize I am not perfect. And they don't have to be either.

What we pay attention to grows – do we worry and fret about things? They will grow to enormity. Do we focus on what we want rather than what we don't want? What do we feel like when we focus on the negative, on our mistakes? We feel down, we feel unworthy, we feel despondent, we feel anxious. We have confirming evidence of our ineptitude. And it becomes easier to find more and more evidence. It's everywhere. When we look for it. When we feel this way, we are more likely to grab the cookie, the chocolate, the remote, the extra glass of wine. When we don't know how to comfort ourselves from the inside, we reach for the comfort on the outside. Shifting our focus is calorie free, keeps us from feeling like a slug, and keeps our mental facilities fresh. Simple? Yes. Easy? No. What we focus on grows. If we continue to focus on what we might not have done well, we will walk around in a state of less-than-worthy and I-should-have. Our inner bitch cowers during those times. In fact, it is more likely that we feel bitchy during those times than like the powerful bitch we truly are.

State it in the positive – not with an unrealistically optimistic viewpoint, but a reframing so we are putting the good out there. By focusing on something, we notice confirming evidence of that occurrence. If we expect people to be kind, we will interpret their behavior as being kind and we will pick up on anything that could be construed in that way. This confirmation bias occurs either way so why not find more evidence for the good? By focusing on what we want, acting as if it is happening, we talk about it more, which leads to others knowing about it which can lead to connections and synergies. And things happen. We begin to get what we want. What we focus on grows.

Pause: Gratitude Journal

When we live with a focus on what we have rather than what we lack, we are more likely to be content. Taking the time to reflect on the many things for which we are grateful will turn our eyes toward plenty rather than scarcity.

This exercise is simple but not necessarily easy. Its simplicity is the challenge. Many of us think that we will do this exercise someday, or that we already are grateful for what we have. Already live in a state of gratitude? Great! Humor me and do the exercise for a month anyway. That will be sufficient time to shift perspective and build the habit.

Find some way to capture your gratitude. Pick what works for you. Some make a section in their journal; others have a specific gratitude journal. A few women I know like to put their statements on sticky notes and decorate their walls or mirrors. You could draw a tree and add leaves of gratitude. You could do the paper chains we made as children. You could simply add it to your daily calendar.

When you have decided what will work for you, commit to writing down three things you are grateful for every day. You can do this at night, in the morning, at lunch. But do it the same time every day so it becomes part of your routine. This is one of the reasons people don't do a gratitude journal/list – because it seems so easy. But it won't get done if it isn't part of your routine. Stack it on to something else you do so it becomes natural. Think of three things while you are brushing your teeth, singing in the shower, whenever suits you. Try to think of different things every day, but don't stress if you are truly grateful for the same thing every day. Sometimes our life is like that. You can be grateful for little things – like the barista who made your coffee, or for air conditioning in the summer.

That's it. That's all that is asked for this exercise. See what a difference it can make in your life.

Feed the Emotion, Starve the Inner Bitch

Food was a vehicle for so many things growing up. The mantra in our house was "I shouldn't eat that. I shouldn't be eating this. I shouldn't have eaten that." Guilt and regret were present even before the food was consumed. It's as if our internal self is overtaken by our desire for and guilt around that food. The mantra, the shroud, is reverently placed over the food – before, during, and after – to demonstrate that we are virtuous, even if we believe our behavior shows otherwise. This is how I (and I suspect others) grew up – believing that food consumption came with judgment. And if that is the case, what does it mean if we are overweight? If we don't match the societal ideal? The mantra acts like an umbrella – covering us from the rain of disapproval, but we often get wet from using umbrellas. When we put up the umbrella, when we put down the umbrella, when we are not completely covered by the umbrella, when the rain splashes inward from the wind. The mantra does not protect us. In fact, sometimes the umbrella does more harm than good.

I began at an early age to associate food with comfort, food with joy, food with sadness, food with discomfort, food with anger…. Well, gee, looks like I began to associate food with all feelings – good and bad. Something good happen? Let's celebrate with dinner and cake! Something bad happen? Let's commiserate with dinner and cake! Going out for ice cream can just as easily be celebratory as compensatory.

Society teaches us that food can be our reward. "I deserve this _____." Fill in the blank with cake, cookies, ice cream, second helping, or glass of wine. When we work hard, when we feel badly, when something hasn't gone right, when something has gone right – all are appropriate times to apply food. Food is a socially acceptable placater of the soul.

But most of all, I learned that food is what I use when I didn't know how to express my feelings, consequently silencing my inner bitch. My inner bitch did not want to use food – she wanted to share how she felt and express herself by dancing for joy, stomping her feet in anger, yelling from the mountaintop, throwing her arms up to the sun. But I was afraid of not fitting in and making waves. I was afraid of the magnitude of my emotions. Food became a salve for the wounds I was developing. I thought that if I fed my emotions, they would be quiet. Have you ever given a child a snack so he/she would be quiet? I think we all have. I think that's why Goldfish® crackers were created. I did this regularly and consistently to distract myself from my negative emotions, slowly burying my inner bitch with food.

And I was successful. I kept my emotions still and hidden, unintentionally quieting my inner bitch. I learned early, as many children do, to hide my negative thoughts. We were taught as children from the very beginning to stop our tantrums, dampen our negative feelings, even quiet down when we are excited and joyful. As if the joy might make us explode or disrupt others. For many children, these messages work and then roll off their backs. For some of us, particularly little girls, those messages are internalized. Our displeasure isn't acceptable; our feelings are undesirable or invalid; and we are too noisy even in the good times. These little girls begin to shrink into themselves; their inner bitches deprived of nourishment just when they are beginning to bloom.

Stuffing my feelings, hiding the storm

I stuffed my feelings inside. I steadily gained more and more weight – until I was near 200 pounds at age 10. Not a great strategy for deflecting negative attention. I retreated into my success – into what I knew would bring a moment or two of positive feedback. But what I was actually doing was putting my head down and focusing on staying under the radar. I wouldn't express confrontational thoughts or opinions. I was protecting myself on the outside, and simultaneously harming myself on the inside.

Agree, stuff the feelings and thoughts. Nod and smile. That became my strategy for keeping the peace. On the outside. But not on the inside.

As an adult I was told many times, you are so calm. How can you be so calm when there is so much going on around you? How can you talk about sending your daughter off to Latin America for a year by herself with such peace and calm? When I was getting married, a coworker had asked my dad if I was excited and he replied that I don't get excited. I'm calm. What? He was right, though. I am even-keeled. On the outside. Always on the outside. Don't let people see you sweat. Don't acknowledge the inner turmoil.

Meanwhile, the hurricanes, the ice storms, the floods, the tornadoes – all were lashing me inside but no one knew. Often not even me. By numbing myself with food time and time again, I lost the ability to know what things felt like – both positive and negative. I didn't let myself feel the joy because of fear of disappointment or something possibly going wrong. And the negative feelings – well, they are too scary. And they might inconvenience someone else.

******

With five kids in my house, control abated chaos. The control backfired for me. I felt like I was continuously under a microscope, with my behavior, attitude, and emotions under scrutiny. I ate to fill the void, I ate to ignore the tension I felt around me. I didn't want to be the focus of attention at all. I didn't want the conversation to have anything to do with me. I wanted to be silent. I found myself being very good about leaving things the way they were, making sure I made no mark. And left no mark. I wasn't only silencing myself, I was making myself partially invisible. And each time, I was burying my inner bitch deeper and deeper.

I see a strong connection with my current self. I am often complimented (criticized?) for how observant I am. I likely developed this skill as a defense mechanism to protect myself from negative comments if I left things out of place. I would scan the environment after I was in it to remove any signs of myself. Silencing and disappearing. The complete opposite of the need to be seen and validated, which helps explain my constant striving to achieve enough to be seen. Do well, accomplish, achieve more so I can be seen. Be quiet, eat quickly, hide all signs of myself so I am invisible. The only way I could be made real is through my accomplishments. All the rest was not worthy. And worse. It should be hidden, made invisible, silenced.

Pause: Out of the Ordinary

Getting out of your ordinary routine is an important part of understanding how you are currently living your life and how you want to be living your life. We often go through our days without even thinking about most of our activities. We are on auto-pilot, moving from one activity, one task, one meeting, to another. And the days go by. Sometimes unnoticed. We get stuck in a routine that may or may not fit with our vision for our life.

This exercise is designed to make you aware of your activities, your choices, and your day. You want to be thoughtful about your decisions; you want to bring awareness to your day. You want to create a growth mindset, getting out of your routine, so you become consciously aware of what you are doing. One way to increase this awareness is by deliberately trying to do things that are out of your ordinary. People typically either love or despise this exercise while it is ongoing. However, at the end of the time period, they often say it was incredibly powerful. Some of the biggest haters chose to continue doing it because it made them really think about what they were doing. It helped them think outside the box – and even be aware of the box itself.

How can you shake up your routine? How can you deliberately create a new mindset, one of conscious choice for your life, rather than same-old, same-old?

Exercise. For one month, do something out of your ordinary every day. While this task may seem overwhelming in the beginning, it takes on a life of its own. The out-of-the-ordinary tasks don't have to be difficult. You can take a different route to work. You can do a different exercise routine. You could take a class you have been wanting to try. You could try a new food. You could commit to saying hello to people for a day. You could talk when you would normally be quiet. Or be quiet when you would normally talk. You could provide water to a homeless person on the street. Anything goes as long as it is something out of your ordinary routine. Thirty days. Definitely do-able.

Take note of how this feels. Journaling about your activity and your reaction, and possibly that of others, is a way to acknowledge your experiences. Looking back at how you felt about this can be a powerful component. Mind-mapping is another way to document your progress. You could take a photo of the out of the ordinary activity, or something along the way if you are taking a different than usual path. Commemorate your stepping outside your box and living your life consciously and intentionally.

At the end of the thirty days, spend some time thinking about your ordinary. Do you want to continue on that path? Do you want to shake it up? Have you found new ways of doing things that you want to continue? Whatever you decide is perfect. It's about making the conscious decision to move in that direction rather than be on autopilot. Doing things out of the ordinary can facilitate hearing your inner bitch and creating new thought patterns in your life. And you may notice that you are purposefully living and enjoying your days, rather than feeling like Bill Murray in Groundhog Day.

The Weight of Emotional Pain

My childhood is an interesting combination of academic success and emotional turmoil, expressed through my relationship with food. Kindergarten was a fun place, where we learned to tie our shoes, memorize our phone numbers written on large construction paper phones, and have a good time learning all the important things we will ever need to know. I lived right next to the elementary school, so school was an extension of home in some ways. The school was my backyard, my playground, my place of retreat, my panacea. Is it any wonder that I began to excel? I should send a shout out to my oldest sister. She insists (and I have no contradictory evidence) that she taught me my ABCs so all of my subsequent success was due to her. Thanks, Barb!

I quickly discovered I was good at this school gig. In kindergarten, I was a normal weight child. I began to get a little pudgy in second grade. Within the next two years, I put on a lot of weight.

I began to deal with stress and unhappiness by gathering provisions. I would store food in my drawer at home, along with all the negative emotions I had, not sure what else to do with them. I stockpiled food – making sure there was something for me to eat if I needed it. I was a junkie, but my choice of drug was legal and socially acceptable.

Food became my primary companion, my comfort, my sole (soul) source of positive experience. I filled my emotional bucket with food – the vehicle I knew best for filling the emptiness inside me. The fullness in my stomach would somehow ameliorate the emptiness in my heart and soul. It didn't work. Perhaps the physical discomfort of a distended stomach momentarily took my mind off my emotional and spiritual emptiness but the metaphorical emptiness remained.

My vessel needed to be filled – the emptiness cried out to me constantly. I wonder now if I had addressed the emptiness if it would have dissipated, vanished. Could I have addressed the emptiness with acknowledgment and empathy? My inner bitch was getting so buried that she would require excavation when I decided to seek her out.

Filling my emptiness with food brought negative attention to me, exactly what I was trying to avoid. Kids chanted "Weebles wobble, but they don't fall down." I just laughed it off, pushing down my sadness and embarrassment. I didn't let others know how much it hurt. I had learned that letting people see they have hurt you gives them ammunition to hurt you again.

What did I do during junior high and high school? I excelled at excelling. I received award after award. But I didn't feel whole. Food remained my best friend. I was still hiding my feelings, silencing my inner bitch. I did not know how to release the pain inside of me. I had not learned an appropriate way to deal with my thoughts and feelings. All I knew how to do was eat, stuffing the thoughts and feelings down. Eventually the anger and the hurt began to back up the pipes. When I began to know more of who I was and began to recognize injustices and frustrations, which often happens during adolescence when one's cognitive development catches up with the rest of the body, I wasn't sure how to handle those frustrations.

Then it happened. I was reading a magazine which was surely telling me how to be a better, more beautiful, fitter, sexier woman. I was 16, seeking answers to how to meet societal and cultural expectations. And in that "be a better woman" magazine was a cautionary tale about a girl with bulimia. Paradoxically, I was attracted to the idea rather than warned against it. For those who may not understand body image and food issues, this is not about being able to eat like a glutton. It was about nurturing myself in the only way I knew how. It was self-care, though misguided. I felt that if I didn't eat, my emotions would cause me to self-destruct. I couldn't handle the emotional, internal turmoil. But food lessened the pain, dampened the internal struggle, and made me feel full, which I mistook for whole.

The bulimia was more about the binging and purging than about the food itself. The binging began to be planned, to be followed by the purging, but rarely was food the impetus. The process was a form of stress relief, of being in control, a way of expressing and getting rid of my negative emotions. I was able to purge them out of myself. I didn't know at that time that binging and purging had to do with my need to be able to understand and express myself, but I knew it wasn't about the food. I did know, in the beginning, that it helped with the "I shouldn't eat that, I shouldn't be eating this, I shouldn't have eaten that" pattern of messaging with which I surrounded myself. If I was able to rid myself of those negative feelings, then I could likely get rid of others. And my journey began.

I struggled with bulimia throughout high school, college, and graduate school – I continued to be very successful academically, and I continued to use food as my comfort and mechanism for control. Food consistently was associated with feelings for me. Feelings I couldn't otherwise have, and I allowed myself to experience those feelings along with the food. It felt safe, because I was in control. And it brought the physical feeling of being filled up – of being complete, whole. Inappropriately filling my self-care bucket. It was as if the gas tank on my car was filled with sludge (negative emotions, stress, and chaos). Binging and purging was a way to fill the tank and then empty out the sludge. Emotionally, I felt free. I had gotten rid of those negative emotions – the sludge. I felt accomplished after the purge. I felt successful. I felt complete and finished. I also felt broken and scared. This wasn't how I wanted to be. I wanted to be free.

Fielding Shame

I had lost some weight as I grew up – before I developed bulimia. Women with bulimia are generally not thin, and it is typically not a weight loss strategy. For me, it may have started as a weight-gain aversion strategy, but it became much more. The weight-gain aversion, though, is a very important part, as it is the hook that draws many in. What does the fear of the weight gain signify? A loss of worth, a lack of acceptance, loss of control, not having it together.

Our society has clear boundaries around what is an acceptable body type and bias against bodies outside those boundaries. Although our boundaries may be blurring, the bias remains. Our ads are now speckled with women who are not stick thin, but overall there is an expectation that women who are thin and muscular have it together and are more worthy than others. And these messages are harmful to young girls – girls as early as 8 years old are dieting and trying to manipulate their bodies to fit the social norms. The desire to fit in, to be accepted, to meet the needs of belonging and esteem is very strong, and our epidemic of eating disordered behaviors in young women, especially, indicates we have a long way to go in accepting people for who they are. And it begins within each of us – by accepting our inner bitch for who she is.

Some may think eating disorders and weight go together. But for me, they are separate. I could be very heavy and have an eating disorder. I could be very thin and have an eating disorder. The eating disorder was not about the food or the weight for me. It was about control, worth, value, self-judgment. It was about not being good enough. Not being content with who I was.

In the same way an alcoholic is always an alcoholic, I venture to say that someone who has had an eating disorder continues to carry with her remnants of the disorder. Someone who has alcoholism can stop drinking. But a person with an eating disorder cannot stop eating. And food, like alcohol, is an ever present mechanism for celebration and commiseration. Food is a socially acceptable method for dealing with happiness, joy, sadness, frustration.

Some of us apply food as one might apply a Band-Aid, covering up the wound so it can't be seen. But instead of the wound healing, it remains dormant, just under the surface, only to reappear. But the Band-Aid only hides the wound; it doesn't heal it. Food will never heal the emptiness, the desire for control in a seemingly chaotic life, the need for validation, the urge to be heard. We have to do that for ourselves – and for each other.

Societal views on food are quite judgmental and biased. From my personal experience, I have noticed if a thin person is seen eating a relatively unhealthy meal or snack, she rarely gets comments or looks. If a heavy person is seen eating the same snack or meal, they will often receive dirty looks or comments. The implicit message is – "You should not eat that. Can't you control yourself? No wonder you are the way you are." As if who we are is how our body looks.

The societal messages are ubiquitous and potent. "Get your body Instagram-ready." "Look good for others." Even "you are what you eat." The range of socially acceptable bodies is narrow. Step outside that range and risk implicit or explicit bias from others. Many women who are outside that range have already learned to feel "less than." Those media bodies who are within range are often air-brushed and photoshopped. We don't see their real bodies, complete with stretch marks or imperfections. So, not only are we being indoctrinated by messages about size and worth, we are being bombarded by messages about flawless appearance, effortless perfection – which is not effortless but is created through hours of professional make-up artistry.

Fielding shame from external and internal sources is exhausting and led to my desire to numb those feelings and to eat. To fill the void. To numb the pain. And when the feelings of fullness begin to dissipate, those negative feelings begin to resurface. It becomes be a cycle of despair.

Emotional pain can be challenging. When I was younger, I really wanted this emotional pain to be external – I could deal with it if I could see it. My internal pain was not legitimate to me – it was not acceptable or desirable. I was only imagining it. I was overreacting. I was dramatizing the situation. At least that's how I felt. I was definitely not in touch with my inner bitch. Although by this time she was literally screaming to get out. But her screams were not heard through the pacifying layers of food. We have mechanisms to deal with bodily pain. When people see someone with an injury, be it a bandage or a cast, they often ask about it, offering condolences and support. Not so with internal pain because it can't be seen unless we are willing to be vulnerable. But being vulnerable comes with risk, since many do not know how to handle others' internal pain. We resort to platitudes to placate the emotion. People mean well, but we are generally uncomfortable in the emotional realm. All one would have to do help the other feel heard and validated is the same thing we do with bodily injury. "What happened? I'm so sorry that happened. That stinks. Is there anything I can do?" But we put up our armor to protect ourselves from others' pain because it makes us remember our own.

Pause: Worry Well

Mark Twain has a famous quote that puts our worry in perspective:

I have had many horrible things happen in my life, and some of them actually happened.

This pause is created for the worriers out there. The idea is to get rid of, or at least minimize, your worry. If you do not worry, then please do not add this activity to your day!

Worry is not a productive activity – it does little but expend precious life energy and create more of what you don't want to happen. The more we focus on what we don't want, on the "what ifs," the more we invite those things to us. The "what ifs," "if onlys," and the always/nevers can wreak havoc on your soul and mind. Overthinking is not a productive past-time; it takes energy and steals your peace. It doesn't provide an outcome. In fact, the best answers often come after you have taken a break and are thinking about something else entirely for a while. The fresh perspective, the rested mind – that will be the fuel for the best possible solutions.

Well, if worrying does not do anything positive, why worry well? Since many of us are accustomed to worrying and often even feel that worry is a productive activity that is necessary for us to move forward, we want to start where we are. I often hear from clients that they think worrying helps them keep their edge, that if they didn't worry they would be less successful, that worrying itself helps them stay on top of things. They tell me they want to stop worrying, sleep better, feel less anxious. Yet, it is not uncommon for us to purposefully bring things up to worry about, as if it is an agenda item for our brains. The least productive type of worry? Worrying about not having anything to worry about. Worrying becomes a habit, a defense mechanism. If I worry about something, then I have a plan of action for all of the "what ifs" I can think of. But it doesn't work that way.

By excessively worrying about an issue or situation, several things can happen. First, we wear ourselves out. Our brains need rest and diversions to come up with creative solutions. Worrying mires us in the situation so we can't see clearly. This makes us less effective when something actually happens on which we need to take action. By not worrying and waiting to see what happens, we have a fresh perspective and can address the situation in more effective ways.

Second, worrying wastes our precious time and energy. We only have so much time and if we are worrying, then we are not thinking of or reflecting on other things. We are not noticing the beauty around us, or engaging with those near us. Worrying is like sitting in a rocking chair – it gives you something to do, but doesn't get you anywhere. Or like leaving your car running in the driveway overnight. It wastes gas and energy, doesn't get you to your destination, and releases harmful emissions.

Third, worry can affect our emotional and physical health. It can prevent us from sleeping well; it can lead us to eat reactively and choose less healthy food options; and it can raise our blood pressure and increase our cortisol levels, both of which are not good for our bodies over time. Worrying can increase our physiological stress reaction. Stress is good for us in short bursts; over time it has kept us safe and helped us act quickly in a dangerous situation. But we are not meant to keep that up over long periods of time. Our bodies and our minds need rest.

Worry becomes a habit. It is a defense mechanism that does not serve us well. Worry is different from planning. Planning is coming up with likely, or possible, scenarios and coming up with action plans around them. Worry is excessively thinking about these scenarios and the many things, likely or not, that could go wrong. Good project planning is helpful; going down the negative swirl of worry is not. Worrying about what other people are thinking is particularly ineffective. Most of the time, others are not thinking about what we did or said anywhere near as frequently or vehemently as we think. We are not as important to others as we think we are.

What does it mean to worry well? It means setting a specific time each day to worry, setting the timer and going for it. Knowing that you are going to worry at a specific time allows you to stop thinking about it non-stop. It also allows your brain to rest so you can focus on other things. When the worrisome thought pops into your head, you are able to say to yourself, "I have time set aside to worry about that. I don't need to think about that right now." Then when the time comes to worry, look at your list and actively worry about the items on your list until the timer goes off. Then put the list away and go about your day. While this may sound contrived and artificial, it allows you to focus on what you need to focus on at that time and to be more effective for the rest of your day. Over time, you will likely see that you don't worry as much during your designated time to worry. You may find that you shorten that time of worry, telling yourself that there is nothing you can do about it so worrying is useless. You will be breaking the habit of worry.

Remember, worrying is different than planning. Planning a trip means that you are thinking about actual details, like getting a hotel room, booking a flight, creating a map of where you are going. All of this is useful and needed. But worrying involves contingencies for all the things that could go wrong and rehashing them in your mind over and over. Worry does not equal action. Worry equals emotional angst.

Exercise: You will need a timer (hour glass, watch, kitchen timer). I prefer something that will ease you out of the time, not blare a siren when your time is up. Although if it is obnoxious enough, maybe you won't want to start worrying because the sound at the end is so bad. You will also need a note pad, sticky notes, or a way to take notes on your phone or other electronic device. You will want to make sure this is something you can have with you at all times so when something creeps into your mind that you feel like you need to worry about, you can jot it down. That way you know it is captured and you don't need to keep it in your mind.

Set aside a time each day that works for you. Preferably the same time every day, but do what works best for you. Set your timer for 10 minutes. That should be enough, but if you are just beginning and you think you can't accomplish all your worrying in this time, feel free to make it longer. You will likely find, instead, that you don't need that much time and are ready to move on to the rest of your day before 10 minutes pass.

This may show you how much time is taken by worrying. It's harder to measure how much you are worrying when you are worrying all day long. But worrying all at one time is much more effective. When you sit down to worry, pull out your list and begin worrying about the items on your list. This is your time, if you must, to say "what if" and go down the spiral of negative possibilities. Then when the timer goes off, put the list away until tomorrow.

Pay attention to the process and to your decreased need to worry. The realization that worry is a habit and not productive is life-changing. The time and energy we used to spend worrying is now released for other activities we choose to do.

Finding Your Inner Bitch

Phase Three: Releasing Your Inner Bitch
Chapter 4: My Life Path

In my Develop Your Life[8] course, I ask the students to draw their life path to understand how an individual's past leads to the present. The first time I did this exercise in front of the class, I was taken aback by what I saw. I had not intended for this to be an ah-ha moment for me. I was simply demonstrating the activity. When I looked at my life path, I was able to see the pattern woven by the threads of decision, choice, even accident. My tapestry was being created, with some threads dominant throughout – even though I was not always aware. As early as my childhood, I wanted to help people. I wanted to write. In fact, I did write – I spent weekends writing. One of my biggest regrets is that I did not save those writings. But I was practicing – without even knowing it. Then I hid that desire – until it no longer could stay submerged. This book within me is coming out whether I am ready or not. I've been working on this book my whole life – it's just that I'm finally sitting down to get the words on the paper.

Many things influenced the me I am today – and I am grateful. Every experience I had, every person I met, every decision I made – they all combined to make me who I am. When I was engaged to be married, I wrote to my then fiancé that I wanted to have a private mental health practice, with an office at home so I could be with the kids and still have a career. That was in my early 20's. I had a vision for my career – and for my work/life balance. In a minute it all changed. I was offered funding for graduate school and off I went to study human development.

Once there, I quickly realized I was not in quite the right field. But I was on a trajectory, one that was fully funded – we had moved to Pennsylvania from Hawaii (!) for me to go to graduate school. My new husband had moved with me and I was fully embedded in the program. I looked hungrily at the clinical/counseling and organizational psychology departments, for a minute, until I resigned myself to sticking with my decision and staying my course in human development. Though I wanted something different, I felt I couldn't change. I felt I had committed and I didn't really know what I wanted. So I ignored those feelings, stayed loyal to a decision I had made, and kept going down my path toward my doctorate in human development.

And yet – looking back – I think how silly that was. My inner bitch was definitely buried at that time. She expressed herself in the letter that I wrote, but when I took the path of least resistance (can one say that about getting a doctorate?) she went back into hiding. Rather than going to the departments and asking what it would take to switch programs, what kind of financial assistance I might be able to get, I pushed down these desires and went forward with my life plan, the one already in motion. My life plan which was created, by the way, by a single phone call one morning in Hawaii. I had applied to only one graduate program, Penn State, before Brian and I decided we would move to the west coast and work while we decided what we wanted next. I was bewildered when I received the call from Penn State – offering me complete financial assistance if I would attend their graduate program. It seemed too good to turn down, so I didn't. We altered our path, packed our bags, put away our vision, and moved to State College, Pennsylvania.

At times, I let things happen to me. Good things. Great things, even. But I followed a path that was created for me, rather than one I designed myself, thoughtfully. So why wasn't I willing to explore my options when I was at Penn State? Why didn't I find out what it would take to alter my path? Because I was afraid of someone saying no. I was afraid of someone finding out that I wasn't quite happy in my path, that I had made a mistake, taken a wrong turn. I should point out that this exploration was occurring during my masters' studies – early in my graduate career. I remained at Penn State for 6 years – if I had earned my masters in human development, I would have had time to finish a doctorate in something else.

In fact – I want to catch myself in that statement – "I would have had time." What does that mean? Time before what? We often put ourselves on an artificial timeline, one that essentially holds us hostage in our decision-making, keeping us on a path in which we feel we have invested too much or that we will be "behind" if we step off it. Life is a journey, with many curves and turns, sometimes even spirals. The destination is artificial. Once you reach it, there is another one right around the corner. And that is what makes life amazing. We often hold ourselves to these arbitrary, even artificial, time standards – believing we need to finish "on time."

Twenty-five years later, I wouldn't change anything in my life path because I learned so very much about myself and about life. But if I could coach my younger self I would help her see that my inner bitch, my true self, was expressing herself, and at the very least, I could have explored those other options to see what they would look like. Smothering those thoughts and feelings were not the healthiest choice. But it would have taken courage to make a change. Probably not as much as I was imagining, but I wasn't confident enough to take the steps to find out. I was afraid of being laughed at, of being told no, of the snickering I imagined would happen when I suggested I might be interested in joining these other departments. Who, you? Why would we want you in our department? Who do you think you are? The irony, of course, is that none of that would have happened, and by not exploring, I found myself in the exact same place I would be in if, in fact, they said no. I share this because my story is not unique. I hear many young women express these same thoughts – fear of making waves, feelings of having already invested in a particular path, having misguided loyalty.

There are many paths to the same place. And each path can be wonderful. Am I glad I earned my doctorate in human development? Absolutely. I am grateful all the time for this accomplishment and for the doors it has opened for me. I love teaching and I likely wouldn't be in North Carolina if I hadn't taken the path I did. I do work I enjoy and find meaningful. And I help people optimize their lives by choosing their own path, the one that is best for them. And I am writing. Again. I was not fully equipped in my 20's to do all of this – even if I had achieved a doctorate in a practicing psychology field.

My focus is different as well. The time is perfect now – and my experience of burying my own inner bitch allows me to illuminate when others are doing the same. This applies to everything in our lives – relationships, career choices, family situations. All things bring us to where we are, influencing who we are at this moment. Opportunities arise at the right moment. We often cannot connect the dots until we look backwards.

My visual life path shows me the moments when I purposely chose a direction – like when I decided in my senior year of college that I really didn't want to be a doctor, a path I had adopted as I see many young college students do, because it is admirable, expected, worthy. And yet, it wasn't me. I wanted to do something great – but I wanted to be me more. I am proud of that decision; I am proud that I heard my inner bitch speaking and I listened. It was not an easy decision. Yet, when I shared that decision, my fear of what others would say or think were unfounded. People were supportive. Others generally want you to be happy. So I was living out a story of pleasing others that no longer fit. Toward the end of graduate school, my inner bitch began to emerge, making a plan for what I wanted and implementing it. I applied for and received a post-doctoral fellowship. I am still here. And yet, perhaps not the way I thought I might be.

I spent four years in college, six years in graduate school, and three years in a post-doctoral fellowship at a premier academic medical center. As my fellowship was ending, I was uncertain about my desire to enter a full-time faculty position. I did a brief job search and did a couple job interviews, half-heartedly. I had two small children at home. Did I want to leave those babies and take a job which would require me to prove myself in the first few years? Not really. I stepped off the faculty career path and on to a wonderful 10-year journey of raising and homeschooling our children. I made a very conscious, deliberate choice about what I wanted for myself and what Brian and I thought was best for our children and family. I thought out the consequences, the value and meaning of this decision. At the same time, I turned down an exceptionally well-paying job as a statistician, of all things.

My doctoral training was very statistics-based, and I am good at numbers. A faculty member saw that and offered me another path.

I was at a juncture. I chose family. Some may have their feathers ruffled because this is a stereotypical female thing to do. However, this is one of the times in my life when I did what I truly wanted to do – what my inner bitch was screaming at me to do. Listening to your inner bitch means doing what you think is best – despite what others want you to do. In this case, I was going against stream, although it looked like I was stepping into the cultural current. Imagine telling your parents and friends that after 13 years of college, graduate school, and post-doctoral training, you were going to stay home with your children. I was an exceptionally well-educated mom.

Decisions are usually not one-dimensional. There are so many things to consider in each decision – and sometimes one aspect of the situation may experience a bit of a loss while other aspects experience a gain. Deciding which way to go can be difficult. Which is why being in touch with your inner bitch, hearing what she has to say, actively seeking her opinion is all so important. We have to make the best decision we can at the time we are making it with the knowledge we have at the time. Oh, how easy it is to look back and say – if only I had done X. Well, you knew why you didn't do X at the time. And you made a thoughtful choice. Have things changed? Likely. But you don't know what would have happened if you had done X. I do know for sure – you wouldn't be who you are and where you are right now. And who you are is complete awesomeness!

When I first arrived for my fellowship, I sought teaching opportunities. Although there were none at the time, it wasn't long before a need appeared. I taught one course a semester for those ten years that I was home with the kids, which allowed me to maintain and nurture my professional identity and be a grown-up for a few hours each week.

And I am so grateful I took the path I did. Sure, we had bumps in the road and I was not a perfect mom, but I don't have any regrets about this decision. Had I taken the statistician job, I might be wealthier, but I could never be richer than I am now. My life could not have been fuller, more authentically lived. And it was an awesome demonstration of how listening to my inner bitch led to a life fully lived. When I review my life path, there are times that I see synchronicity – the right pieces all fell into place – and it is how I know that my inner bitch was leading me and I was listening.

Another pivotal moment occurred in March 2005. I will go into more detail about this moment a bit later, but for now, I will say my world collapsed in an instant. Many years later, I can see the beauty in the tragedy. The darkness of that time allowed the light to appear even more strongly, creating the colorful, visual pattern of my life. I knew that my inner bitch was leading me through one of the most difficult times in my life. When all of the societal expectations were stripped away, my inner bitch was able to express herself. She came out of hiding in the rubble. She knew what to do. She took over when I was numb and in shock. My inner bitch and I became one.

That moment led to other moments on my life path, including ending our homeschooling journey and going back to work full-time, which gave me many opportunities to exercise my inner bitch's muscles. We sometimes can only see the importance of events, decisions, comments by looking retrospectively. That is when we see how we silenced our inner bitches or how she guided us when we listened.

Pause: Trace Your Life Path

Exercise, Tracing your Life Path, Part One

For this exercise, you will want to have some colored pens and a good size piece of paper. Sketch out your life from the beginning to where you are now. Think about the decisions and influences. How did one fork lead you to where you are? Who showed up along the path?

Mark the monumental, memorable events, remarks others made that left an impression, transitions in your life that may have seemed inconsequential at the time but led you a certain way. Some events may seem like nothing – don't judge. Just add them. You will look at the big picture later. The dots may connect; they may not. But getting your life picture down is critical to finding your inner bitch. Tracing your life path can help you understand the past as a bridge to the present and a gift for the future.

Your line can be straight, curved, of even a series of spirals. One of my retreat participants traced her body and put her life path inside the tracing. Be creative and have fun.

Exercise, Tracing your Life Path, Part Two

After creating your path, answer the following questions.

  - o Are there threads that appear throughout your life that work together to create the tapestry that is you?

o Looking back, do you see times when your inner bitch shone through?

o Are there times when you can see her hiding a bit more under the covers? Are there times when it is obvious that she is hiding? Times when she was dormant?

o What influenced either of those times?

o How did you end up where you are? Can you identify the sources of reinforcement in your decisions? The internal motivations for your decision?

o What did you bring to each environment you have been in? How did you intentionally or unintentionally create your environment?

o Do you see recreations of your experiences? Perhaps manifested in different ways? Do the same challenges reappear in different situations and contexts? Is it possible that you draw out these challenges, that you bring them to the context? How do you keep recreating the same experience by thinking the same thoughts, telling the same stories, and doing the same things?

When you look at your life path and consider these questions, remember that what you experience today is a result of choices you have made in the past. As you think about the choices you have made, consider that you can change your thoughts, your direction, and your behavior. Are there changes you want to make with regard to these?

****

It's awesome to think about how you might show up on someone else's life path. What are you doing that might make a difference in someone else's life? What are you saying that might propel them forward? How are you helping someone else find and nurture her inner bitch?

Out of the Rubble

Easter 2005. We had our annual Easter party on the Saturday before, to which we invited about 60 people. The morning of the party, we painstakingly surveyed the backyard – looking for every possible danger point. We removed sticks and trip hazards. Yet, there was a hidden danger that we could not see.

The adults hid hundreds of eggs, released the kids for the hunt, and excitedly watched from the deck. After the hunt was over, I gathered the children at the front of the house to admire their bounty. The front door was open. I heard a loud noise – looked through the house and saw heads disappear, literally disappear in front of my eyes. I was confused, wondering how that happened. The deck had collapsed. It felt like my whole world collapsed in that instant.

I ran back to see everyone lying on the ground. A friend had blood dripping down her face. In my state of utter confusion and disbelief, that felt like a recognizable, manageable injury. I ran back inside to get a towel when I heard someone yell that my mom needed me. I ran back and saw the scene differently this time. I really saw it. It looked like a bomb had gone off – the rubble, the bodies lying on the ground, with a few sitting up – my mom laying ashen on the ground. Her coloring definitely not normal. Her first hoarse words to me were, "How did we get into this mess?" Good question, Mom. We did everything we could to protect people – and yet, here we were in this mess.

In the background I hear our doctor friend giving instructions on what to say to 911 – multiple down, send multiple ambulances. Some other gobble-de-gook but my attention was splintered across multiple stimuli – the bleeding that needed a new towel, the people holding up the deck so it didn't swing back down, the sweet neighbor children who brought a home first aid kit to help, my mom who was mostly silent, a few children crying in the background. Someone needed a pillow. A swirl of sounds, sights, emotions.

And then, blessedly, the sound of sirens. I remember feeling – thank God, someone will come and take control. I can rest. I was wrong – yes, multiple ambulances, multiple fire trucks filled the cul-de-sac, but I couldn't rest – not for a long time, actually. But I didn't know that at the time.

They put my mom on a stretcher and carried her up the hill, almost falling when they stepped into another danger spot – a small divot in the yard. We shared an ambulance with a neighbor – both level 1 trauma – the most seriously injured. We were whisked away to the hospital. I was frustrated that they didn't use their sirens and that they had to stop at every light, which caused our passengers to cry out in pain. I was frustrated at how bumpy the ride in an ambulance was – and every bump led to more cries of pain. My mom kept complaining that her arm was falling and could someone please put her arm back on the table. Turns out her shoulder was shattered, so her arm was essentially detached from her body. I was so glad when we arrived because they could finally administer pain medication to bring some relief.

We sent six double-occupancy ambulances to the emergency room that afternoon – moving other patients into the halls. It was surreal to be in an emergency room and know most of the occupants. "It was my house" became my mantra in the next few hours, and days. I remember desperately wanting a Diet Coke. A couple came to visit and check on me, which was so sweet. They asked me what they could do for me – I asked if they could please bring me a Diet Coke. They said yes, but they didn't return. I am not sure what happened. Did they need to go home? Was this a Pepsi location? Not sure. I just remember looking forward to a brief moment of relief – in glimpse of normal routine and caffeine – a small moment of refreshment that never came. Silly, I know – but it impacted my perspective moving forward. I incorporated this lesson into my life. I now operate on the premise that it is often the small things that can make a big difference for someone.

At one point, my friend who had been bleeding walked in through the ER door, with her head bandaged, reminding me of a bunny. I was tickled by how cute her bandage was, particularly on this Easter eve. The juxtaposition of intense sorrow and momentary happy joy in seeing her was an oft-felt emotional cocktail that day, or night. Not sure which it was. Day/night is indistinguishable at the ER – time loses meaning – except for the time between pain medications and doctor's visits.

I was told I had to get the ring off my mom's finger or they would cut the ring off. I spent at least an hour trying everything I could – ice, soap, gel, and prayers. I finally got it off. The irony is that the more I worked to remove it, the more the finger swelled and the harder the ring became to remove. A good life lesson – sometimes overworking a problem or an issue makes the solution more elusive. Swelling takes up more room, making the issue harder to deal with. And the best way to get rid of swelling is rest, ice, compression, elevation. All of which require a pause, which we are often hesitant to take. The task gave me something to focus on – a goal I might be able to achieve amidst a sea of chaos and trauma.

Finally, around midnight, a room became available for my mom. We were in the elevator – the nurse, my mom, transport, and me. The nurse asked me what happened. I told her – my delivery not matching the severity of my words. And then I said my mantra, "It was my house." Four little words that changed the story, and truly my life. The nurse looked at me, really looked at me, as if she could see into my heart and soul. I remember nothing about her, but I remember her words, "Have you eaten?" Those three little words permeated my glass bubble. I don't know. Had I? I think I ate breakfast that morning. "What do you need? You need to take care of yourself, too." I need to take care of myself, too.

Suddenly the tears appeared. The emotions surfaced. I hadn't cried yet. I had held it together. I had felt nearly every possible emotion in the last 18 hours – excitement, joy, love, happiness, then – fear, anxiety, sadness, horror … – but only superficially for the negative ones. I couldn't afford to feel them deeply. Or I would break into a million pieces. They had to wait. I couldn't tear my clothes and wail like I really wanted. I was the one not hurt. I was not on the deck. It was my house. It was my house. It was my house. How did we get into this mess?

When we got settled in my mom's room, transport came to take her for an X-ray. I stopped them as they began preparing her for the trip back down. She had just had an X-ray in the ER and the trip to her room was traumatic and painful. She needed to stay where she was, I said. She needed an advocate. She needed someone in touch with her inner bitch. That had to be me. My inner bitch took over. She was the advocate, the one who stood up to the system. Many times people trust the system, believing it knows best. My inner bitch said no. Check with the ordering doctor. See if this is truly needed. And then come back and get her if so. My inner bitch stood her ground.

Crushed shoulder, liver laceration, brain bleed, most of the ribs in her back broken. My mom was in the hospital for five plus days. We made the local news and CNN – my brother heard about the accident in Oregon. There was a picture in the newspaper of Brian talking to my dad – who had to hear that his wife of 50+ years had dropped 12 feet to cement and was tenuous at the hospital. I don't remember how or when I went home to check on the kids only to turn right around to go back to be with my mom.

My tribe

An army of angels. When the accident happened, I was peripherally aware of what was going on around me. Of guests packing up food – of people comforting children, of those who sat with the injured, of some of the injured themselves who, despite their serious injuries, helped hold up the deck to keep others safe. My attention was torn – I wanted to check on all of them – I wanted, irrationally, to help clean up – but I sat with my mom – while I seemed to watch everything from above – not in a metaphysical way but in a hyperaware way. Aware of it all – my people-pleasing side trying to take care of all things but my inner bitch planting me firmly where I needed to be.

As my mom was being loaded into the ambulance, I glanced toward my children and had to decide in that moment where I would go. I couldn't be in two places at one time. I didn't have the luxury of time to explain to my kids – to offer comfort. I never asked – I just knew in my heart and soul that they would be cared for. My friend looked at me as I entered the ambulance – and I knew. I could go. I was released from those ties momentarily so I could be with the one most vulnerable at that time. In swooped my army of angels. Amanda was taken to a friend's house at which an Easter basket appeared for her the next morning. Our sons, Brayton and Ben, were watched by a dear friend at the house.

My friend stayed the night – explaining to the boys where we were and responding to doorbells from reporters wanting a statement. Grammy and Pop Pop left to come to us. I'm not sure when they arrived but they dropped everything to come. I'm not sure how the door got boarded up or how everything got cleaned up. But it did. We received numerous phone calls from well-intended friends. 'I hear your Easter party was a smashing hit." They, of course, did not realize the extensive damage to person and property.

A friend bought me a cell phone – so I could be reached. A tool for connection - truly a thoughtful gift. My sisters mobilized to help care for my mom when she was released to my house from the hospital. Friends took my kids for hours on end – accepting them into their family and allowing them to be kids while I tended to my mom. Without my tribe it would have been much harder. I couldn't have been where I needed to be. They bolstered and supported me, both practically and emotionally.

While undoubtedly a tragedy, this event changed my life. I had to get to know my inner bitch better. I had to trust her. I had to let her take over when I was numb and in shock. And this was the beginning for me – the beginning of realizing what I had been missing. Because I was put in a critical place, I didn't have room for the noisy roommate – all is stripped away when things really matter, so why can't we get rid of the negative self-talk, expectations, and doubt during our daily lives and decisions. I had to rely on my inner self and my own truth. Life is short and can change in an instant. Out of the rubble can come beauty. And it did – in the form of my inner bitch.

Pause: Reflect, Breathe

The best and most beautiful things in this world cannot be seen or even touched – they must be felt with the heart.
– Helen Keller

I cannot think of an exercise that would honor this event in the way it deserves to be honored. I would like to ask that you take this time to look around at who and what is in your life. Hug your family members, be grateful for the people in life. Life is tenuous, and difficult things happen to all of us. Life is messy. You get to be part of the mess. Life is what happens each and every moment.

Take some deep breaths. Savor a sip of coffee. Enjoy a bite of dark chocolate. Appreciate the smell of a rose or the sweet smell of a baby (if you know one – people don't like strangers sniffing their babies). Let someone know you are grateful for him or her. Reframe the events in your life so you can see the value in them. Pay attention to the way the sunshine is sparkling on the trees.

Just be. For just a few minutes. And pause.

Growing up Together

I married young – before I graduated from college, at the age of 21. I would not recommend getting married that early because young adults are often still figuring out who they are. But we got lucky. We are still married after 32 years. We grew up together in our marriage, and we allowed each other to grow individually. Sometimes marriages fall apart because one grows and the other stays the same – or they grow in different directions. We ebbed and flowed, but our marriage was the container in which that happened. We were (and are) two individuals with differing developmental paths that were developing within the context of the marriage. It worked for us – was it easy? No. Worth it? Absolutely.

I believed the myth that we would settle down and know exactly what we wanted and who we were when we became adults. I craved that certainty. Now I realize it is a work in progress and always will be, with confidence and competence increasing over time. I remained uncertain about who I was and I still had not learned to effectively express my negative feelings – my anxiety, my insecurities, my anger. And now, being in a marriage, it was confounded and compounded. Marriage is a transition, when both individuals are asserting their selfness while trying to become a couple. Maybe this doesn't happen in other people's marriages, but we argued when we were first married. And that was scary. We weren't supposed to argue; we were in love. We were supposed to live happily ever after. We had achieved our childhood mandate – we had found the partner with whom we were going to settle down and have a life. What does that mean? How does one "have a life?" Where is the instruction manual? Think about the messaging our society gives us about relationships. We either see the ideal, romantic side (particularly in jewelry ads) or we see the divorces of various celebrities, delivering the message that either there is intense joy or there is failure. There is a whole world between those two extremes. Marriage is a like a marathon, one for which we are not well trained. We just start. And we need nourishment and care along the way, just as marathoners do.

Our societal expectations influence our views. When two people decide to get married, they are in love and everything is supposed to be rosy. Happily ever after. Except for when it isn't. There is a lot to figure out in a new marriage, and if children come into the picture, then that makes it even harder. My inner bitch was trying to surface, as it was beginning to get a bit of air after I decided I didn't want to be a doctor, after I moved out of my childhood home and began to experience my own self. But I didn't let her fully express herself. I kept her hidden most of the time out of fear of myself and my emotions. What if I got so mad or sad or even happy that I couldn't contain myself? What if I exploded from emotion? I was afraid of expressing myself. I hadn't learned how to do it – I wasn't sure if I could do it. I don't think I was aware that I wasn't doing it. It had become a habit, a way of life. I was so used to putting others first. I didn't know what I wanted. I didn't know how to live a life that was not wrapped around achievement and success. I didn't know it was possible.

Early marriage was a time when I was bitchy, not authentically releasing my inner bitch. What? How can that be? Finding your inner bitch is about being your authentic you, it's not about marking your territory, making sure your ideas are heard no matter what. In our early marriage, I was more concerned about being right, being in control, than I was about figuring out ways we could both thrive. I was jockeying for position, often resorting to bitchiness. Not my finest moments. The struggle for control in my marriage was an outward manifestation of the struggle for control in my inner life. I wasn't sure who I was so I was definitely not going to let someone else tell me. I struggled to find the balance. Fortunately, we waited six years before we had kids, giving us time to find the balance, the "we" along with the "me." Here I was – a woman with a PhD, teaching at a premier university, who by external measures had it all together. And everyone thought I did. But I was not at all in touch with my inner bitch. I quieted her regularly, shushing her out of fear.

With help and work, I was able to begin the recovery of my emotional self and say goodbye to my bulimic behavior. I no longer want to fill my emptiness with food. I do not want to cover my inner bitch – I want her out in the open, fully expressing my emotions.

The Shadow Child

The birth of our first child, Brayton, broke our hearts wide open, creating an intense vulnerability like I had never experienced before. The overwhelming feelings of love and awe took me by surprise, but I willingly stepped into the wind tunnel of emotion. I consciously relished the emotions I was feeling and fell deeply in love with each of my three babies (Brayton, Ben, and Amanda) and who they were to become.

I grew up with my children. And it was through my children that I began to pay more attention to myself. And particularly, when my daughter was born, and I looked into her sparkling blue eyes and saw that sweet little inner bitch, untainted, unhidden, unsilenced, looking up at me, I knew I needed to learn how to live as an emotionally healthy, empowered female so I could help her do the same.

Okay, you say – that makes no sense. Women don't begin to pay attention to themselves when they have kids. I did. Because now the stakes were high. My own emotional health and development were critical since it directly affected our little ones. For me, it was the process of teaching my children to express themselves – that their emotions are valid, that feeling a certain way is simply feeling a certain way – there is no judgment in feelings – that helped me understand the same for myself.

Through teaching my children these things, I began to teach myself. I was a shadow child, along for the ride. The little girl inside me, the one who began so very early to hide her feelings, listened as I empathized with, nurtured, and validated my children. In very important ways, I was empathizing with and validating myself. I was allowing my inner bitch to get free, slowly, over time, in small ways at first, and then in bigger ways. I began to stand up for myself, not in the bitchy way that I used to do at the beginning of our marriage – when I felt I had to be right and mark my territory. Instead our children taught me, through my learning with them, that I can get what I need while the other person can get what he/she needs. There is enough or all of us. The more we give, the more there is.

This is not an idealistic, all-is-well picture. I struggled. In a few short years, I navigated an accelerated emotional development path learning how to express my negative emotions, from infancy to adult, starting with the screaming toddler that was not allowed to have the tantrum. My poor children. I know I overreacted to some things, perhaps many things. I was sometimes more upset than the situation warranted. They learned very young that mommy says "I'm sorry." I made mistakes, and I owned them. I wanted them to learn to express themselves. I am sure I could have done a better job, that I stifled them in some ways, that the parenting pendulum shifted in other ways. But I am forever grateful that I learned how to express myself with them. They provided feedback for me. How I felt when I spoke with them in different ways was immediate feedback for the next time. When I was able to express myself calmly and firmly, I felt much better than when I was reactive. When I allowed my inner bitch to express herself, I didn't need to waste time and energy feeling badly because she knew how to express herself appropriately. And over time, I began to figure out more about who I was and what I wanted.

If you struggle with this, it is my hope that you can learn to do this now. Taking small steps, beginning to express yourself, becoming aware of what you need and want. All of these can be started right now. Because your inner bitch will be in control – she won't let you self-destruct. She wants to be free. She wants you to be free.

Pause: Incremental Expression

Become aware of times you defer to others and begin to use those opportunities to express yourself. Slowly build on your ability to express your feelings calmly, not letting them bottle up until you feel like you will explode. Assert yourself in small ways at first, testing the water, especially if you have internalized the belief that your feelings or desires are less important than caring for others.

Begin stating what you want in all things. It becomes habit for us to defer to others. It seems like it is either – we are responsible for coming up with the plans – or we defer to others. For example, many women feel like they need to be the ones who come up with the meal ideas. In practical experience, when I have asked others what they want to eat for a meal, I get answers like "I don't care." "Anything is fine with me." From the outside, this looks like flexibility. But in practical terms, it is delegating responsibility for meal planning and this can become a burden for women. So it may be a matter of stating that you are not deciding. That might be how you express your inner bitch. At the other end of the spectrum is our tendency to defer to others when making decisions, like where to go for dinner, or what to do for fun. It's the little decisions that we defer to others regularly that keep our inner bitch hidden.

Exercise. Find times in your day that you would normally defer to others. Journal or mind map those times and consider what would happen if you expressed your thoughts or desires. The next time a similar situation occurs, experiment with expressing your views.

Make a conscious effort to make decisions that express your preferences. Become aware of times you defer to others and use those opportunities to express yourself, even if you do not have a strong preference. This will allow you to become accustomed to saying what you want.

Awareness and incremental expression in small things will help you feel more comfortable when the stakes are higher.

Journal about how it went – and celebrate your courage.

Colorado River

In order to heal my emotional self, I knew I had to develop a healthier attitude toward food. I have heard many say – think of food as nourishing your body. You need to feed your body the fuel that it needs. I am in complete agreement with that. But I also believe food can nourish your soul and your spirit and accepting and embracing this is important. And my inner bitch digs me some honey barbecue potato chips occasionally.

The first thing I needed to do was to replace that mantra: "I shouldn't eat that. I shouldn't be eating this. I shouldn't have eaten that." I had spent years hearing and repeating those few sentences. Think of how a small rivulet of water can become a stream. I had a stream (think Colorado River) flowing through me that felt all kinds of guilt about food. I slowly began to pay attention to what I wanted to eat. Really pay attention. I began to believe I could eat whatever I wanted when I wanted it. This is counter to most of the weight loss strategies I have seen over the years. But dieting is about deprivation and loss. As soon as the 'diet' and deprivation was over, I would release the food flood gates. I knew that would not work for me. Instead, I began retraining myself in an unconventional manner. I began to consciously immerse myself in the world of plenty to heal my feelings of scarcity.

Nothing is forbidden. All food is good.

My excavation of my childhood story that food is dangerous, we have no control over it, and it somehow makes us consume it without our consent ("I shouldn't eat that, I shouldn't be eating this, I shouldn't have eaten that") began in graduate school. I knew I had to develop a healthier relationship with food and with myself. So began my unconventional training, the conscious immersion into the world of plenty, rather than scarcity and deprivation.

I began carrying a candy bar in my backpack, with the explicit instructions to myself that I could eat it anytime I wanted as long as I replaced it immediately, so I always had a candy bar with me. It was there for me to enjoy; I gave myself permission to indulge when I wanted. Unorthodox? Yes. But this process of knowing that I could have whatever I wanted and that there was always more began to release me from feelings of scarcity and deprivation. I began to live in the world of abundance and slowly I no longer wanted the candy bar.

Though I ate it frequently in the beginning, I eventually threw away a year-old candy bar. I had retrained my thoughts and actions. I began to understand I did not have to have guilt around food, and I could eat whatever I wanted when I wanted it. And the 'want' became clearer and more distinct. I stopped eating it just because it was there. I ate it only when I truly wanted it. I also began to not finish the candy bar, throwing it away after a bite or two, knowing I would be able to have more the next time I wanted it. Consciously immersing myself in the world of plenty healed my feelings of scarcity.

Essentially, I catered to that little girl inside me who wanted to make sure she had her provisions, in case she needed them. I worked with the emotional and behavioral scaffolding I already had. I took baby steps toward healing those thoughts and behaviors. Cold turkey doesn't work for me. When I am deprived, a whole set of reactions begins, including an intense desire for whatever it is that I'm not supposed to have. Regardless, I began where I was. I set my intention around what I knew worked for me.

This process enabled me to get in touch with what my inner bitch wanted and release the negative feelings I had about food. I no longer considered any food forbidden nor did I try to substitute one thing for another. I'm done with trying to substitute celery for potato chips because they both crunch and the celery will satisfy that need for crunch. I have eaten way too much celery, only to be followed by most of the bag of potato chips. I have had to trust my inner bitch when she says she wants her honey barbecue potato chips. And then pay attention to how much she really wants. It was usually not as much as I would eat when I ignored her.

Negative emotions still make me a bit uncomfortable, but I have learned to allow my inner bitch to express herself in healthy ways. Most of the time. What happens in childhood is extremely powerful and is not easily overcome. And food still has meaning beyond nourishment for me, as it does for most.

The mind is a powerful tool. Leverage it.

We are all three-year-olds at heart. They lack conservation, which means they don't understand that the properties of an item don't change just because we change the shape or the size of the container. In other words, if a three-year-old is unhappy with the amount of ice cream you served her, you can, in front of her eyes, put the ice cream in a smaller container so it looks like more, and she will be happier. We can be childlike in this way – we can use smaller serving dishes, using our visual sense to satisfy us. The average dinner plate has grown in size over the years, as have portion sizes served at restaurants. A serving size of ice cream is half a cup. Have you ever served yourself half a cup of ice cream?

Our average bowls would make half a cup of ice cream look like one spoonful. Putting it in a beautiful small bowl helps me feel decadent and magnifies the experience of eating the ice cream. This is not about restricting myself. It is about **not** restricting myself. For me it is about building in checks and balances so my inner bitch – the part of me who is aware of what I am doing – remains in control. For me – it is not about the serving size. It is about paying attention to my enjoyment. A small amount is often enough. This took me years of carrying a candy bar around and replacing it, retraining my mind and heart about food. (There is more to this story, but that has to be another book.) It didn't happen overnight, but when it happened, it stuck. Because I changed my thoughts, which changed my beliefs, which changed my actions, which changed my habits, which changed my life. Truly.

What do I want? What do I need?

I feel like my life is two distinctly separate chapters – the overweight chapter and the non-overweight chapter. I look back to that very heavy child and feel great sorrow for her, but I don't feel like it was me. I'm not sure if that is because I am not sure who the real me was, or if I look back and can't see her as me. Or maybe I don't want to. Maybe I don't want to claim those very unhappy feelings. They are still a little scary for me. Even after all these years and how far I have come, I am still a little afraid that if I felt all those bottled up feelings I might explode or implode. I know – they are all a part of me. I am grateful for all I have gone through, because I have a very deep empathy and understanding of emotional pain and emptiness. I come from a different place now. I come to these feelings in the moment, mindfully. What do I need now? This is much easier than thinking about the entirety of those emotions bottling up.

When I am tired or not caring for myself in any number of ways, I am less adept at making thoughtful, conscious decisions. I revert back to habit mode, or to mindless munching. I am not sure I will ever 'arrive' in the sense that I will be completely free of that. And that's okay. A version of the 80/20 principle is my overarching guideline. If I can be mindful and conscious 80% of the time, and nudge myself higher continuously, then I am doing well. My inner bitch wants me the whole me to be healthy.

Pause: Your Oxygen Mask

If you have flown before, you may have heard the flight attendant to remind you to put on your own oxygen mask before your child's. You are not able to adequately care for others if you are not getting enough oxygen, consequently putting both of you at risk. By caring for yourself first, you are able to think clearly and breathe deeply as you care for others. This is an essential component of allowing your inner bitch to thrive. It is also often the first thing sacrificed.

There are many fun and meaningful ways to engage in self-care. This exercise is ongoing – refer to this list regularly. Add to this list as you go – the possibilities are limitless. You could also put these ideas in a jar and pull one out when you want something spontaneous. Just as the options are many, so are the types of people. Not all of these will fit your style – that's great. Pick what you like and what is meaningful for you.

**Find your anthem(s) – a song that inspires and moves you. I listen to several anthems regularly. They are empowering songs that feed my spirit and encourage me to stay tapped into my inner bitch. Listen to them, sing them loudly, and/or dance to them. My anthems are:

- "Masterpiece" by Jesse J.
- "Unwritten" by Natasha Bedingfield
- "Fight Song" by Rachel Platten
- "Brave" by Sarah Bareilles
- "Roar" by Katie Perry
- "Turnin'" by the Young Rising Sons

**Find time in your day to check in. Even a few minutes can center you if you pay attention to what you need at that time. A five-minute break every hour, a walk at lunch time, anything that fills you. The important aspect is that you are paying attention to you, asking yourself how you are doing, and caring for yourself in the moment. A conscious shift in perspective helps anchor you in your day.

**Develop a mantra that motivates, inspires, centers, or balances you. A mantra is a positive statement that you repeat to yourself to remind you to be mindful and live intentionally. For example, I often tell myself, "I am peaceful and calm." Or "I am a priority in my life."

**Practice meditation. Meditation can be a meaningful way to bring consciousness and intention to your life. There are numerous wonderful resources on meditation, some of which can be found in the Resources section.

**Read or listen to books/podcasts that you find meaningful. I enjoy reading books like *Gifts of Imperfection* by Brené Brown or listening to podcasts like "10% Happier" by Dan Harris. See the Resource section for suggestions.

**Give yourself the gift of time away occasionally, whether it is for an hour (for those with small children) or a weekend. Consider a retreat weekend to allow yourself to refresh and recharge. *Sol Searching* retreats offer an opportunity to reflect on and recharge your inner bitch at the beach (see Resource section).

**Spend time in nature. Find a local arboretum, garden, beach, hiking trail, or park and be reminded that we are but a blip in the world. Nature has a way of centering and grounding us, reminding us that we don't have to control everything. It has its own natural patterns and forces. Tides go in, tides go out. Trees drop their leaves to allow new growth. Beauty abounds.

**Exercise. Engaging in physical activity is good for our bodies, hearts, and souls. Putting on a good sweat is a great stress reducer. If you don't like exercise, find something fun to do – pickle ball, kickball, hiking, cycling, or tennis. Engaging different sections of the brain and body lets the over-used parts recover. I ~~love~~ like to go to spin classes where I can engage physically and check out mentally.

**Color! Adult coloring books are everywhere now. I still like the kids coloring books though, as they are less stressful (ha!). Either way, coloring engages your left brain allowing your right brain rest. Coloring can allow your true self to emerge – or at least to have a chance to be heard. Your inner bitch can peek out behind the shadows while your analytic/judgmental brain is dormant.

Exercise. In addition to indulging in the above activities, spend some time considering the following questions.

• Mind map or journal how you care for yourself in less-than-healthy ways. What are some less-healthy ways we engage in self-care? I snack when I am tired. I have also been known to watch more than one episode of Grey's Anatomy at one sitting. The activities themselves may be fine; it may be more about how much you do or why you do these activities – such as avoiding or numbing feelings.

151

- How can we find healthy ways to care for ourselves? Make a list of things you like to do or may like to try. Incorporate these self-care activities into your routine.
- Create daily self-care, weekly self-care, monthly self-care, annual self-care goals. Remember you are worthy of the investment. Caring for your self is an integral part of keeping yourself healthy as well as enjoying the days you are given.

Chapter 5: The Industrious Inner Bitch

Doing meaningful work is important – it helps us be purposeful, productive. Work can mean many things – I view time in school, high school or college, as work. Our work environment can be part-time or full-time. It can be paid or unpaid. Work is an arena where we practice all the things we learned in kindergarten – sharing, communicating, waiting patiently, getting along with others. It may also be where we continue hiding our inner bitch or release her and let her shine.

What am I worth?

I began watching other children when Amanda was a year old. The idea was brought up by our mailman, odd as that sounds. I believe life and opportunity happen when we are being ourselves. There is a Zen saying, "How you do one thing is how you do all things," that symbolizes this for me. Who we are as people is evident in the way we act when we are being ourselves. People notice and make connections (or not) based on those observations. When the children were very small, we played outside a lot and we would leave cold or hot drinks in the mailbox for the mailman, often with a package of home-baked cookies. And we would chat when we were in the yard when he came by. He and his wife were expecting their first child and he asked if I would be willing to babysit.

That opened the door of my mind – I didn't watch the mailman's baby – he lived too far away to make it convenient. But my inner bitch was evident in my negotiations with the parents. I wrote in my journal about my fear of asking for a fair rate – for what I was worth as a woman with a PhD in human development who was homeschooling her children. Several days' worth of journal entries were dedicated to how I hate to ask for the money, but I was going to anyway. My inner bitch wanted me to stand up for myself, to get paid my worth. My noisy roommate was causing me to doubt my worth. I had the conversation with the parents and my journal entry from that day says they didn't blink at my rate, which shows me that so many of our problems are imaginary, big in our minds but non-existent in others'. I inflated my importance in their mind – not that I egotistically decided I was more important, but rather, that I conflated my concern or worry so that I projected unto others my own feelings of doubt. If only I could have all that time and energy back. But I can't. I can, however, limit the amount of swirl I engage in now and in the future.

The idea of watching other people's children was now in my mind – the door opened further when a friend asked if I would consider watching the new baby of one of her colleagues. My inner bitch grew again as I walked into their house and asserted myself with regards to my babysitting fee. Money is one area where we commonly hide our inner bitch. Women are generally afraid to ask for a fair rate, for raises, for promotions, for what we want in the workplace. We feel less than. Our noisy roommates ask us, "Who are you to ask for that?" We cover our inner bitch with the insecurities that have been indoctrinated into us by years of silencing and societal messages.

But every time I had the money conversation, I could feel the glow of my inner bitch as she grew bigger. I didn't always get what I wanted, but even if I didn't get what I wanted, I was successful. I had expressed my needs and/or desires. I could then choose whether what I was being offered was worth my time and energy. And I didn't explode, implode, or otherwise deconstruct when I was told no. We so often build up the fear of being told no or having our ideas rejected; we even sometimes feel shame if we are told no. We need to recognize asking for what we want or need and working toward getting it is a success by itself. Most of the time it is not a black and white no or outright rejection. There is a lot of gray area in negotiations. We want to build our negotiation skills, be willing to ask for what we want, and realize that if we are told no, we are in the exact place we were before we asked.

(I do not always hear my inner bitch or follow her directions. I still worry on occasion about what others are going to say or think. I still worry about failure or making a fool of myself. But now, my inner bitch walks beside me and holds my hand as we walk through the situation together.)

I negotiated my babysitting fee and subsequently watched that baby for three years – she became an important part of our life. We still see and love her. She led to another baby and then another. By this time, Amanda was four (or so). I began watching this last little one when she was about ten months old and watched her until she went to kindergarten. This child also became one of our family and remains dear to us.

As she was getting ready to go to kindergarten (to learn all the important things in life), I was offered a research job. All arrows led to this career juncture – the deck accident had happened the prior year, we had spent much of that year suffering from PTSD and navigating personal conflict in the home, the baby was going to kindergarten, and one of my children wanted to go to "real" school. With everything pointing in this direction, I took the plunge and reentered the full-time, outside-the-home work world.

The metaphorical playground

I became a full-fledged adult, or so I thought. I learned more about my shortcomings and how I often buried my inner bitch at work because I was unsure of myself, I didn't want to make waves, or I felt obligated to put others first. The struggle became real as I had to choose between work and the family sometimes. Sometimes I was unclear what my responsibilities were and how far I had to take them. Other times I focused on my strengths at work, which made me an excellent employee but put me in conflict with what I wanted to be doing at home. My strong sense of responsibility was a detriment to my well-being. I felt like the buck stopped with me – that I was responsible for the success of work projects. I also felt responsible for the success of my children. But I was able to temper that some of the time. I knew they had to go through things on their own, but I had to wean myself from being the rescuer. It did not happen overnight – in fact, I am still waiting for it to take hold, but I am getting better.

I found work to be a metaphorical playground where I had to figure out the rules of the games. When could I stand up for myself, when did I have to put others first, when should I speak up, when do I take a seat at the table? How do I let my natural leadership tendencies flourish without stepping on toes or squashing other people? I erred on the side of staying quiet, not voicing my opinion, staying in the background as I observed the workings of the workplace. I wonder – do men ever feel this way or think these things? Is this a byproduct of my socialization and the stories I carry with me? I think so. I don't think men spend time ruminating over these kinds of questions. I had serious neural pathways in my brain developed – new context, same thoughts, same behaviors.

I found I struggled with certain personalities, particularly when it came to saying no. There were many situations which I thought were inherent to the work place, that if I were to leave it, my life would be much easier. I struggled with this even as I grew in my career. As I became surer of myself, I didn't gain the corresponding ability to consistently stand up for myself. I often put my own needs behind someone else's. I became flexible and easy going – on the outside.

I hid behind the façade of flexibility. Flexibility as a front for insecurity. Mostly because I was worried that I might be viewed as demanding or that the other person wouldn't want what I wanted. Which I now know is ridiculous. I did it to myself. I sat on the sidelines of decision-making when I could have let my inner bitch express herself more. And that became a slippery slope. If I'm not willing to assert what I want in small things, how am I going to disagree about something in a meeting? I agreed too often for the sake of self-perceived peace and protection.

The Imposter Syndrome

I brought along my childhood stories to work, and with them I also brought the feeling I was not good enough. The Imposter Syndrome is felt by many successful, accomplished people, regardless of gender. It is the feeling that we are going to be found out to be a fraud; that we are not as good as others think we are; that we have been lucky so far; and that no matter how qualified we are, it is not enough. The Imposter Syndrome can lead to excessive overworking, preparation, and worrying. It can also prevent us from taking advantage of opportunities because we don't believe we are good enough yet. We still need more training, more experience, or more degrees.

Women often will not apply for jobs unless they meet 100% of the job requirements. Men, however, will apply if they meet 60% of the requirements[9]. This can be attributed to a lower level of confidence in women, as well as a lack of understanding of the hiring process[10]. Women's hesitation to apply to a job for which they are not fully qualified may be due to the fear they won't be able to do the job well or they won't be hired because of their lack of qualifications –they aren't good enough yet. Men also claim the latter reason for not applying for a job, but they still apply for many more jobs than women. Women would be well-served by understanding their limiting beliefs, acknowledging their feelings of being an imposter, and embracing their imperfections.

The roots of the Imposter Syndrome run deep, with underpinnings in our childhood. For example, when we are told we are smart (or given a trophy) without earning the accolade, we may begin to wonder when others are going to see the truth about us, because we have somehow fooled them. Oh, the irony – the ways we have tried to increase self-esteem in children may have contributed to a deeper, pervasive sense of self-doubt.

Whose expectations?

In the workplace, I felt like I needed to produce to prove myself, just like I had when I was in school. I felt I was never enough, I never did enough, and I had to work harder to ensure they didn't discover I was really not as good as I appeared. Back to the old adage from my childhood, "We expect nothing less." Therefore no matter how much I do, the expectations are not exceeded, because the expectations are nothing less than I accomplish. For a woman like me who has a strong achiever and responsibility orientation, this is a difficult battle. Work, work, work. Push, push, push. Strive, strive, strive. And get to the same place of met expectations.

You are likely not tooting your own horn about the good work you are doing. Because it is simply expected. Nothing special, right? We need to embrace our inner bitch and let her proudly share the things we have done. If you are in a supporting role or a behind-the-scenes leader, then it is likely that much of what you do is hidden, because the better the job that you do, the less visible it is. Your work is seamless; there are no hitches or struggles for anyone to see because you have ensured they won't happen. Your work, by definition, has helped silence you. Women are not good at highlighting their successes or their accomplishments. We can get into an unsatisfying cycle of working hard, paving the path and clearing it of debris, while wiping the sweat from our brow, without others knowing what we are doing.

A job change highlighted that I brought this upon myself. I was internalizing an unreasonable amount of responsibility. In fact, I was tapping into one of my greatest strengths. Responsibility is a particularly challenging strength because, on the outside, it looks like a tremendous asset. Employers and managers want their employees to be responsible and to take initiative. But for those of us who are high on the responsibility strength, we may struggle with determining what is enough and what is too much. It's hard to hear our inner bitch telling us to decrease our intense feelings of responsibility. And yet, when we do, everything works out. We have balance, we get our jobs done more productively and effectively, and we don't burn out.

Your inner bitch's voice

Expressing your inner bitch means being true to yourself in whatever environment you find yourself. It means standing up for your team, getting what they need, setting boundaries and realistic expectations. It also means holding your team accountable, while building a culture in which all are willing and able to express their inner bitches.

Learning to communicate effectively and assertively is important for the expression of your inner bitch. I've been in rooms with people who speak over each other, interrupt, and create verbal chaos by trying to out-speak one another. While not pleasant, it has been a learning experience – sometimes one needs to speak up, to be willing to interrupt, to speak over, if one wants to be heard. Depending on the situation, perhaps you will not need to interrupt but become adept at finding the infrequent pause between phrases which indicates a need for air. That is the time to insert self. However, there are times when being willing to interrupt is the only way to be heard. Choose thoughtfully, and then insert yourself as warranted.

You will want to take a seat at the table, literally and figuratively. Pay attention in meetings you attend. Women often sit around the perimeter of the room if there are chairs set up, naturally deferring to others. Take that central seat at the table. If someone needs you to move, they will ask. By taking a perimeter seat, you become part of the outside, allowing yourself to be hidden. It is much harder to be willing to speak from the outside.

The empowered inner bitch speaks out when she has an idea. How many times do we sit with an idea, internally judging it before we express it? Sometimes sharing an idea leads to other ideas, which leads to progress. Our idea may not be the one chosen, but speaking it helps others think as well. We get used to hearing our own voice; and we, as well as others, begin to take us more seriously.

Our inner bitch also wants to speak out when she disagrees. Ah, so much harder than the previous attribute. Contributing an idea is relatively riskless. But disagreeing with someone can feel confrontational. But we don't need to see it that way. Divergent ideas and thoughts make the group's product better. Learning to voice disagreements in a way that acknowledges differing views and presents a new thought in a safe way is an important skill and can be practiced. If you feel uncomfortable with this, practice with a friend, a coach, a mentor, or a family member.

Also, think about environments where you feel more comfortable expressing disagreements. How does it work for you? Are you successful? If so, why? If not, why not? What stories might you be bringing with you from childhood about disagreements? Some families do not encourage, or may even discourage, disagreements. Beginning in a small, incremental way will help build this muscle, just like weight lifting does your physical muscles. Over time, you will be letting your inner bitch express herself at work, allowing work to be a place you feel whole and fulfilled.

Pause: I Can See Clearly Now – Developing your Vision

We have talked about our past and our present; both can now inform the vision of the future. Understanding what we loved to do as children, knowing what makes us feel whole and energized, listening to our inner bitch as she tells us what she wants – all help us create our vision.

By creating a vision for yourself, describing where you want to go, you preliminarily decide, in your subconscious mind, how your future will be; you set the process in motion and take the first step. You allow your subconscious and conscious selves to work together to bring the vision forward. Without a vision, you will not know if you are on the right track or if you need to recalibrate. You will not know if you are living according to your own plans. This exercise specifically addresses your vision for your future, which will help you step into it as if it were already true.

We can easily get lost in the world's expectations and unspoken rules, easily forgetting what we want for ourselves, what makes us happy or feel alive. We can get so busy that we don't think about the big picture, the purpose of our lives. We don't think about what we are here to do, because we are so busy doing. The busyness and cloud of expectations can make it hard to hear the guidance of our inner bitch which keeps us moving in our chosen direction.

Exercise, Step One: Your Passion

Exercise. How does you find your passion? Your journey to finding your passion begins when you focus on what you love to do without thinking about the obstacles that keep you from doing these things. What do you love to do? What do you wish you could spend your time doing? What do you want to do on weekends or when you have a few hours to yourself? When you dream about the future, what do you think about doing? Ignore any obstacles you think may get in your way.

A good way to find your passion is by doing – trying things, exploring and experimenting. Your passion is not always the thing that is going to bring you money. Sometimes your passion might be the way you spend your free time. It is okay to do work you like, that you find meaningful, and then pursue your passion outside of work.

Mind mapping is a good way to think about your passion. Start by putting yourself in the middle and then come up with as many things as you like to do as possible. Avoid any judgment at this point – you are simply free thinking. Include things like eating, baking, hiking. People create jobs around these activities. When one of the mind map bubbles interests you, take that bubble and put that in the center of another mind map. Then brainstorm all the potential things you could do around that bubble. Remember, your passion may not necessarily be your job. In other words, we all have work we are intended to do in our lives – it is truly our life's work. Some of us get paid for it; others do it in our free time. And sometimes opportunity knocks and we get to create a career around our passion.

It may be helpful to project yourself into the future 5 years, 10 years, 20 years, 50 years. From your vantage point today, what are the most important things you are going to devote your time and energy to in your lifetime?

Exercise, Step Two: Your Incremental Vision

Mind map or journal the answers to the following questions.

- o What do you really want?
- o What are your plans?
- o Where do you want to be in five years? (For a few minutes, forget the path you think you should be on.)
- o Where do you want to be in ten years?
- o Are there steps you could take now to get on that path?

Exercise, Step Three: Envisioning the Future

Let your creativity loose in the form of a vision board. Think about what you want and find pictures that represent those things, using either the traditional method of finding magazine pictures and pasting them on poster board or leveraging the internet to find your images. I like this method because I do not have access to a lot of magazines and the magazines I do read are about food. I can only have so many pictures of cake on my vision board!

I have long-term as well as shorter-term vision boards. I have my "ultimate" vision board of what I want to have in my life. Then I have a vision board for this year. I am inspired when I look at my vision boards, and I also ask myself, "What's my progress? How can I move this vision forward?"

There are two components to vision boards. The first may be considered "woo-woo" by some. If we envision what we want, we are more likely to get it. There is a strong metaphysical component to putting what you want out to the universe and being more likely to get it. Some also call this prayer. See, that's the thing. None of this is new. And it is not necessarily mystical or off-the-wall. You will never get the meal you want at a restaurant if you don't ask for it. You will not be allowed into another lane if you don't let the other driver know you want to merge. You have to let people/the Universe/God know what you want, and believe you will receive it. If you don't believe you will receive it, you are sending mixed messages. It's like praying to God about something you want, but believing in your heart that you don't deserve it so why even ask. Do you really think God doesn't know what is in your heart? You have to ask and believe. This allows your subconscious to begin working to make it happen.

The second component is directly related to believing you will get it. You see – if you put it out there that this is what you want, you also need to take the steps to get there. If I believe I will have a beautiful beach house in my future, I need to spend some time looking at beach properties. I believe in serendipity, but I also believe that we have to work toward our vision. If I had a vision I would receive my PhD but didn't apply to graduate school, I would not have been successful in achieving my PhD. By putting your vision on paper, you are declaring this is important and you are working toward it. You are going to do your part to make your vision come to fruition.

Looking at my vision board regularly makes me think about it and live into it. There are times when my noisy roommate chimes in – "Who do you think you are to do that." And I just look at my vision board and remember that I believe in my vision. I step into it, even if I have to step firmly on my noisy roommate's foot!

A note about envisioning your future – please combine this forward-thinking approach with living for each and every day. Everything we have worked toward up to this point is about being your best you. That is for today and tomorrow. Live, love, and laugh today! Don't wait for tomorrow. Always think about the most important things in your life daily, while you are working toward being your best self and living your best life.

Striving or Thriving?

We are accomplishment-seeking beings. We set goals, we achieve them, we move on. We rarely pause to celebrate the accomplishment, basking in the glory of "look what I've done" before we set the next goal and begin striving again. This is important to consider as we think about what the goals mean to us.

We can become single-minded about a goal, set on achieving it at the cost of other things. Some goals require single-mindedness and a bunch of stick-to-itiveness. But what are you putting aside for that goal? Will you be satisfied when you have achieved it? Or will the next goal be immediately behind it? Ask yourself, can you live your life fully at the same time, as you pursue these goals?

I have observed that many people set audacious goals, which is awesome! And they think that when they achieve that goal, then they can exercise, spend time with family, read a good book, have lunch with a friend, go for that walk, etc. You get the idea. Sometimes we put life on hold to accomplish those goals. The goal is reached, and we feel – empty. It is often an anti-climax. In fact, sometimes it is even less than that. It is nothing. It is – okay, finished with that – what's next. At least an anti-climax involves an awareness of accomplishing the goal. Climbing a huge mountain is rewarded by an incredible view at the summit. Submitting a paper for publication feels great when you hit the "send" button, but then there is the next paper waiting to be written. In some ways our technological society has taken even more away from goal accomplishment. I remember the days when we had to print and mail our grant proposals to funding agencies. There was something very satisfying about seeing

167

those hundreds of pages, crisp and beautiful, ready to put in the postal package. Sealing the package, putting your hands on the package to wish it well. Those were tactile moments of celebratory recognition of a job well done. Now we compile it on our laptops, combine pdfs, attach to an email or put into an electronic submission system and hit the submit button.

What the heck is the point of all of this? Should we stop setting goals? No. My point is two-fold. The first, simpler point is to make the time to celebrate our accomplishments. Mark the moment. Make sure it gets on your life path – even those goals that seem small. We focus more on lack than abundance. Focusing on the abundance of goals accomplished, jobs well done, products developed – will bring us more abundance. Figure out what makes you feel celebratory and do it. Make a list of your accomplishments and take a moment to add each accomplishment when it happens and relish how it feels to add it. Tell people who care about you. Create a success ritual. Do whatever you need to do to acknowledge the achievement, to make it real. And pause, even slightly, before thinking about the next one. With each celebration, your inner bitch will glimmer a bit more.

My second point is more challenging but oh so fulfilling. Integrate your goals into your real life. Continue having lunch with friends, make time for that walk, and remember you have a whole life when you are working towards goals. Small goals are one thing – putting some things aside to accomplish the goal is less impactful. But big, time-consuming goals – waiting to live until we accomplish them means we may be waiting to live a long time due to our tendency to find another goal right after one is accomplished. I think of the balance between career and family. How many times do we think little of skipping the bedtime story because we have a deadline? Or working late so we miss the soccer game? Or not taking the time to play the board game (do people still play those?)? But we will do it right after this deadline, or paper is submitted, or project is finished, or ….

My point is that there is always another deadline, paper, project waiting. And unless we consciously live our lives while we are working toward those goals, our lives can quickly pass us by. And our inner bitch will remain hidden and quiet. Set goals. Work to accomplish them. But be thoughtful and conscious about your decisions and your trade-offs. Some opportunities are gone forever. We are rarely aware of an event's final occurrence. We often only recognize it in the rearview mirror. The last time your child wanted to sit on your lap. The last time she asked you to color with her. The last time you snuggled in bed before sleep. Those moments slip away – that is part of growing up. But having lived fully allows us to be more peaceful about the moments passing.

If you are of a certain experience (age), you may have had the opportunity to live on much less than you live on now. You may have thought that when you earned a certain amount, everything would be better. Then you reached that amount. A new amount became the new "everything will be better when" number. And so on. I look back to graduate school, when together Brian and I were living on my graduate school stipend, an amount that seems unimaginable now. We were eligible for and signed up for WIC and free dental care when our oldest son was born.

And yet, as many will say, those were good times. I don't remember feeling deprived. We lived within our means and were able to buy and pay off a house (a very small one) during graduate school by paying a little extra every month. When we earned more, we spent more, and we thought when we earned even more everything would be easier. And so it went. This is similar to goal collection. When we finish X, when we write Y, when we achieve Z, then we will truly live our lives. We humans have become goal setters, or at least we have been trained to be over the years in our society. We were originally hunters and gatherers. Those traits have been subsumed into hunting for the big kill and gathering the rewards. Each achieved goal can easily and quickly be replaced by another, bigger, harder to reach goal, resulting in a life of "never quite there."

Goals are good – having aspirations is important. But living to achieve, to acquire, to accumulate may not be so good if it prevents us from truly living our life. While we often make goals to spend more time with family, read more books to our children, spend more quality time with friends and family, etc. These goals often take the backseat to the measurable accomplishments, such as letters after one's name or dollars in the paycheck. We need to be thoughtful, mindful, and conscious about our decisions. This may seem like the minutiae of life, but it is the minutes that make up the sum of our lives. It is often the minutes that we squander or fill with an achievement or measurement orientation.

We work harder and faster to get "somewhere," but that "somewhere" often isn't enough or satisfying so we continue on the treadmill, reaching for something that seems unattainable. As long as we keep that focus, it remains unattainable. We are looking for satisfaction, for what is enough, for winning the race. But all of that is self-defined. And until we make the conscious choice to consider our own definitions of those terms (enough, winning, satisfaction/contentment), we will continue seeking the unattainable, the moving target of accomplishment and achievement. What race are you trying to win? Who are the potential losers?

We are all given the same amount of time in a day, days in a week, and weeks in a year. We often think about our days in terms of time. I encourage you to also think about it in terms of energy. How much is your time worth? How much is your precious life energy worth? Where do you want to spend your energy? How can you renew your energy? Working non-stop, on the perpetual treadmill, will deplete your energy. Rest is important, maybe even more important than work, as it offers us new perspective, allows us to be fresh, inviting new thoughts and ideas.

Pause: Words to Live By

We often find ourselves living on the daily treadmill, the one that keeps moving, giving us the illusion that we are going somewhere, but in reality we are working hard to get to the same place. While we may move forward and achieve our goals, we may do so in a semi-conscious manner, half-aware of what we are doing, operating on auto-pilot. Our life literally becomes pedestrian. An antidote to being on autopilot is to consciously become aware of what we want in our lives. To live purposefully, create your own story by purposefully thinking about what you want your life to look like.

Exercise. For this exercise, you will want your sketchpad, pens (preferably colored), index cards or some other small paper, and a jar. Spend some time thinking about the words you want to make sure are in your life. What? Words in my life? How do I have words in my life? We already have words in our lives. Anxiety. Stress. Love. Fatigue. Joy. Health. Sluggishness. Family. Loneliness. Some of these words come uninvited; others have been thoughtfully added. We want to grow the list of words that is thoughtfully added. You can do this in a number of ways. You can mind map what you want your life to be filled with, putting you in the center of the page and your chosen words surrounding you. You can make a list of as many words as you can. (See Resources for a list of words.) You can put the words directly on the index cards.

Word embodiment. Organize your list in a way that suits you best. I like to put the words individually on an index card and put them in a jar that makes me happy. A blue mason jar does the trick, probably because it reminds me of wild flowers. Put your twelve (or as many as you have chosen) words into the jar. Each week, pick one word out of the jar. Your task for the week is to embody that word in as many ways as you can, at least one new way a day. This exercise is fun to do with friends. Your word for the week is adventure? Try to eat something new and a little exciting. Go rock climbing at the nearby rock climbing center. Go on a hike somewhere you haven't been. Your word is gratitude? Spend time every evening making a gratitude list, thinking about each item/person/event for a minute or more, capturing your feelings around each one. Write a note to someone thanking them for something they have done for you. Comfort? Get a great book you have been wanting to read and a cuddly blanket. Spend some time curled up reading that book. Wear your most comfortable clothes one day. Wear comfortable shoes to work. You may find you walk more that day also, which would also embody health.

Be creative – think limitlessly about the words. You can think of new meanings for them. Listen to your inner bitch. She has amazing ideas! Recruit a friend to participate in your activities. Your ripple effect will grow and you will be letting other inner bitches shine as well.

Capture the moments and memories of the words, through journaling, pictures, a vision board – whatever your inner bitch wants. This is a perpetual exercise. You can revisit the words over and over, you can come up with new words, or you can spread a word over a month. I suggest starting with a week and building up to a month if you choose. Small successes build larger ones.

Deadlines and Urgency

Conscious living, intentionally choosing what you will do with your time, will help you make better decisions. Thoughtful planning and decision-making can facilitate a richer life in the midst of deadlines. And awareness of the frequency and intensity of these deadlines can help you understand whether this is your way of being or simply a short season. Paying attention to your workload, your list of goals, your "I'll be happy when…" or "I'll play with the kids when…" or "We'll take a vacation when…" statements will allow you to see your own patterns.

You may find that you are in a perpetual series of urgent deadlines. Begin to think about how you can reorganize your time. Do you tend to do the smaller, task-oriented items first, such that they take up more time than needed? Work will fill whatever space you give it, with small tasks taking up most of your time. Focus on your priorities first. Lean into a new work pattern, slowly changing what you can and seeing how it feels. If you work in a group over which you have any influence, suggest creating realistic timelines, getting ahead of the game rather than chasing the proverbial tail.

What is your inner bitch telling you? Are you working smart? Are the deadlines unrealistic? Is this something you are bringing to the workplace through the stories you have been living? Or is this part of the job? We create our own reality through the thoughts we are thinking, the stories we continue to live out. Take some time to think about your work habits and beliefs.

We all know colleagues or friends who complain they have way too much work to do and they can't get it done. Yet, we see them spending a lot of time at the coffee machine, chatting at each other's desks, going out for long lunches. We have to be honest with ourselves as well as with others when it comes to the lives we are living. We need to have our own power and change what we can. And the first thing to change is ourselves.

Some of you may be considering a career or job change. I would encourage you to think about your life in terms of life energy and answer the following questions:

- How much energy are you spending on this job?
- Specifically, what is it about the job that you don't like?
- Is this something you can change?
- Is this something you can live with?
- What is the likelihood that the things you don't like will be present in other jobs as well?

I have coached women who have been unhappy in their jobs, thinking that a career/job shift is the only way to overcome these feelings of discontent. But when they mind map, journal or talk about the specific things they don't like, they sometimes realize that they bring these things to the work place, or that these qualities are just part of having a job. Sure, we all may want more flexibility in our lives, more free time, less busy work. These things are inherent in having a job, and are present in every job to some extent. Even entrepreneurs and the self-employed experience these feelings to a greater or lesser degree at various times. I'm pretty sure farmers don't always want to get up in the dark and begin tilling their land, but it's a necessary part of the job. We don't experience feelings of accomplishment if work is easy. Work is called work for a reason.

It is important to uncover the source of your discontent or dissatisfaction. For me, as I mentioned before, I had pinpointed that I was tired of always feeling like I was responsible for making things happen, for being the one who picked up the pieces, who made sure all the t's were crossed and the i's were dotted. Guess what? I changed jobs, and I experienced the very same discontent, because I brought these things to the job myself. I was living out my story and blaming external circumstances, rather than allowing myself to rewrite the story. Once I realized this, it was easier to change my thoughts and beliefs, because I was aware. I had to be aware first, and only then could I actively work on changing my thoughts and beliefs.

Urgency and fervor can be good in small doses. They motivate us to finish tasks. But over time, they can steal our joy, our energy, and eventually chunks of our lives. Many of us bring our work home with us and the line between work time and personal time becomes blurred.

For the next few weeks, pay attention to your schedule. What did you work on each day? How much of your day was meeting deadlines, with a sense of urgency? What kinds of decisions did you have to make in order to meet those deadlines? Did you eat lunch at your desk? Did you skip exercise? Did you say "later" to your child when she asked you to play with her or tell you about her day? Did you put down your phone at dinner or when talking to a friend? What is your inner bitch telling you about balance and deadlines?

Pause: Mastering the To-Do List

Time is what we want most, but what we use worst.
– William Penn

Many women, young and less young, have shared their challenges with their to-do list. Either their list becomes their master or their list becomes a marker of their productivity and thereby their inherent worth. Their day is measured by their to-do list. I may be the only one who has done this, but I have been known to add something to my list which I have already done just so I can cross it off. Yikes. What does that say about how we measure our productivity and success?

Women have also shared their tendency to keep moving the things on their daily to-do list to the next day, because they haven't gotten to it. It becomes an endless cycle of "less than" for them because they didn't accomplish what they set out to do. They may be focusing too much on the small tasks, not attending to their priorities.

Exercise, Part One: Master To-Do List

This exercise may help if you have either of the above challenges. The task is to make a master to-do list. Take a large sheet of paper, do this on your laptop, or use multiple sheets of notebook paper – whatever you think would work best for you. Dump all of the things on your mind on this list. And I mean ALL things – grocery shopping, work tasks, carpooling, lunch with friends, catching up on the book club book, finishing your taxes, and so on. I do it by categories because that helps me think of all the open loops that are taking up energy in my mind (and ultimately in my emotional life since they contribute to my feeling guilty). I include my priorities, my big tasks, my midsize tasks, and my minutiae. Keeping the big priorities on the list ensures that I pay attention to them. Seeing the minutiae next to the priorities offers perspective on how I am living my life.

I like to use a large sheet of paper and use different colored pens for each category, because that makes it fun. Making my list more concrete energizes me. Having random thoughts swirling in my head that I can't always access exhausts me. I know there is something I am forgetting but I can't remember what it is. I spend my time waiting for the proverbial other shoe to drop. Having it all written down decreases this negative energy expenditure.

When I have all of the items written down, I go through them and think about what is long-term. I have some tasks I know I need to do but I also know I am realistically not going to get to them in the near future. And that is okay. I'm setting my intentions around when I will do these tasks. But having them captured on my list frees me from having to keep them in my mind – which is valuable real estate.

This master to-do list is a living document, with new things being added as I think of them. It is not meant to be pretty – mine has additional notes all over it. Sometimes one task is broken into several parts because it needs to be occur in steps. I find it valuable to do this every two weeks or so, keeping the master list fresh and relevant.

Exercise, Part Two: Daily To-Do List

Then I create my daily to-do list with this list as a reference. And it is important to do this realistically. What am I really going to get done today? If your daily to-do list has more than five items on it, you will likely not get them done. Writing three things down and accomplishing them may be better than taking those two things you know you really aren't going to do and transferring them to tomorrow's list at the end of the day. What is it that is keeping you from doing those two things? Do you really need to do them? Is there fear behind doing them? Are they just annoying? Can they be delegated? Do you really just have to do them to get them out of the way? These are important decisions for those items that move from list to list, day to day.

Exercise, Part Three: To-NOT-Do List

Setting your intentions includes creating your to-not-do list. Some of the items on your master list may ultimately be removed, because they do not belong to you, they are something someone else could do for you, or you are going to be okay with not doing them. As Bill Gates has said, we overestimate what we can do in a day, a week, a year. We underestimate what we can do in ten years.

Be realistic about what you are going to do, what you can do, and especially what you want to do. Don't fill your days with obligatory 'let's do lunch' meetings if you aren't compelled to get together with that person. Look at your list carefully. The list is your vase – the vessel of your life. Don't keep obligations in your vase, at the cost of other more important things. You know those people in your life who repeatedly say 'I haven't heard from you in a while. Let's get together!" Then they don't contact you to schedule a coffee or lunch, but rely on you to make the arrangements. If you find yourself scheduling several of these encounters, you have become the Activity Coordinator. It may be time to quit your Activity Coordinator job. Consider putting that on your to-not-do list and think about what and who makes you feel complete and fulfilled. Spend more time doing those things with those people.

Cognitive Shift

Inner bitches find ways to get our attention if we don't listen. Are you prone to illness or injury? Do you have trouble sleeping because of what happens in your days?

I experienced two instances of inexplicable inflammation in recent years. The first was my ankle. I did not twist it; I did not turn it; I did not injury it in any known way. The doctor and physical therapist were perplexed by the amount of inflammation and how long it took to go away. At the time I was experiencing some challenges in my daily life. I internalized the difficulty. Result: swollen ankle. My support system for my body, my mode of transportation – disabled. Everything became harder. And I am certain it was related to my lack of standing up for myself. My inner bitch relocated to my ankle. Now, I love my inner bitch and she loves me. In fact, she loves me so much that she had to take action to make sure I listened to her. And our inner bitches will do that. They will take steps to make sure they are heard, one way or another. Sometimes we get really good at ignoring them, but once we realize she is trying to communicate, we become more in tune with her messages.

The second instance was inflammation in my knee. My orthopedic doc said – "Oh, you are at the right age. It's arthritis." But it was enormously swollen and incredibly painful, not following the typical arthritis pain path. It was waking me up at night, as if some invisible force was stabbing me with a knife in all areas of my knee. I spent nights on the recliner, because I couldn't put pressure on the knee lying down.

I went to a holistic physical therapy program. Again, the therapist was very surprised by the severity of the inflammation and pain. I could not do the basic tests –

walking so many yards within a certain time limit, getting up and down from a chair without holding on, knee bends or squats (yikes!). I failed. For an achiever like me, that was pretty devastating. The funny part of the appointment was when he tentatively suggested we look at other areas of my life, that maybe we could look holistically at the problem. His hesitancy at suggesting there might be a deeper issue made me smile.

Because by the time I walked (or hobbled) into his office, I had already made the mind-body connection, and I told him I wasn't surprised at all. My knee was only a symptom. A symptom of the chaos I was experiencing. I am convinced that insufficient sleep and high stress levels were causing the inflammation. I am grateful for the inflammation in my knee. I believe it protected me from the silent inflammation and stress reaction that may have eventually led to more serious conditions.

I needed to take action, to listen to my inner bitch. I began to consciously and mindfully release responsibility for those things I could not control. I began to pull back on the drive for accomplishment. This had to be a time of healing.

I took a two-pronged approach to my healing. I began an anti-inflammatory diet[11] so I could identify what I was eating that might have been causing or exacerbating the inflammation. And I believe more importantly, I began the anti-inflammatory cognitive shift, which I devised for myself. I actively began releasing the negative feelings I was harboring. The feelings of responsibility to fix things, to make everyone happy. Every negative thought that entered my mind, I replaced with a positive one. I took a short-term view. I thought about what I needed to do every day. I did what I needed to do to take care of myself daily. I took the time needed for myself, to write in my journal, to recognize my own power. I got down to essentials. I looked at what I was carrying in my metaphorical backpack. And I reached out. I reached out to those I knew could help. I was no longer going to endure this battle alone. I understood my limitations. I listened to my inner bitch.

And, truly, within a week, the inflammation in my knee decreased dramatically and noticeably. My physical therapist was amazed. The combination of the anti-inflammatory diet and the anti-inflammatory cognitive shift was life-changing with regard to my health. I could do the basic tests with flying colors. I once again became the achiever. ☺

My knee and ankle are now both healthy. My inner bitch feels heard. I am continuing the anti-inflammatory cognitive shift – this will be my long-term plan. It is a continual process, releasing and retraining my thoughts so I let go of unhealthy false beliefs.

Pause: Move the Marble

We have patterns that come into play when we enter a situation based on our previous experiences, our stories, our internalized messages. Every time we think a thought, the pattern is reinforced, and it becomes stronger and more pronounced. Like the child's marble game, where the marble stays on its designated path, our thoughts will automatically go to the cognitive pattern we have created over time. Unless a path is purposefully crafted outside of the pattern, unless the marble is consciously moved to another path, it will continue down that path and it will do it all again the next time.

Do we know what the path is? Are we aware of the habitual thought processes and action segments we follow? Most of the time we are not aware. Patterns are very strong motivators for behavior. We like what we know. Much of what we do is subconscious, with very little thought invested. Nature is like that as well, with repeated actions influencing growth.

The Grand Canyon, for example, started with a small stream of water, a rivulet, which eventually created a giant canyon – the power of routine, the power of consistency, the power of habit. We need to consciously create a diversion for our thoughts – an alternate path. We need to change the pattern of our stream by changing our thoughts.

How do we do that? Gently. We acknowledge our thoughts and then purposefully replace those negative or limiting thoughts with other thoughts. We acknowledge that many of those limiting or negative thoughts are from our noisy roommate or from stories that no longer fit us. Then we focus on replacing those thoughts with new and improved thoughts and beliefs.

Where do we get those improved thoughts? We spend time deciding what we want. We make ourselves a priority and decide what we want to think about and what we want to focus on. We sit in silence, we choose quiet for a short time every day. We play in the mud, frolic in the surf, blow bubbles with kids (or yourself). We allow our brain to rest. We allow our soul renewal. We take time away from the distractions which call out to us, which demand our attention.

We give ourselves the distance we need – we consciously move our marble from the habitual path to our new, purposeful path. We deliberately put an obstacle in the river, forcing the water to go another direction. Slowly, over time, the creek will grow and become its own river.

The exercises in this book work together to facilitate this process. Understanding your story, tracing your life path, defining your vision, embodying words to live by, discovering your strengths, celebrating your uniqueness, rethinking your 'mistakes', excavating and nurturing your inner bitch, silencing your noisy roommate – all will provide new thoughts and beliefs with which you will, over time, move the marble.

As you move through these exercises, keep a running list of the negative statements you tell yourself. You will have to begin to pay close attention because your noisy roommate is very noisy. She talks to you constantly, and some of it is not pleasant. There are consistent messages she provides you that may be so subtle that you will have to pay close attention. They are almost subliminal, part of the background, since you hear them so often. It's like that pile of papers that are on your desk that you don't even see anymore because they have been there so long, but they still take visual and mental energy by being there. Bringing these messages to the surface is an important first step to calling them out and replacing them.

Identify your false beliefs, your limiting statements that you tell yourself. To help you, I can share some of mine.

"Why would anyone want to read your book?"

"Who are you to write a book? What makes you special?"

"You shouldn't say anything in this meeting. Other people are more expert than you."

"They are finally going to find out you are an imposter."

I could go on, but I think you get the idea. I am working on creating new rivulets, new patterns, in my thinking so I can change my beliefs and consequently my actions. When I think a limiting thought, I am less likely to believe I can be successful in whatever action it is, which keeps me from acting, which then ultimately affects my life. All because my noisy roommate is working on creating the Grand Canyon in my head and heart! But I am equipped to reframe those thoughts now that I can recognize them. I gently say, "Ah, there you are. I am no longer going to accept that thought. Instead, I am going to think this one." And over time, I begin to believe it and adapt my behavior.

You can, too. This is an incredibly powerful practice. One that is lifelong, since our noisy roommate has a hard time being quiet, and she won't move out. But the more your inner bitch feels free to express herself, the more your noisy roommate's comments will lose their impact.

Exercise. In your journal, keep a running list of the negative statements or stories your noisy roommate tells you. On the next line, write a new statement, a conscious retelling of the story you will use every time you hear yourself say the negative statement. This mental shift will create new, empowering stories over time, stories that will enable you to live the life you want, unencumbered by your own limiting thoughts.

1a. Limiting belief/negative statement

Example: I need to learn to do yoga before I can go to my first yoga class.

1b. Retelling of that belief

Example: It is okay if I am not good at something. I am there to learn.

Setting Intentions: Filling your Vase

Living intentionally, choosing our activities consciously, are important aspects of living in alignment with our inner bitch. Some of us have for too long taken the path we think has been laid out for us (even if we are unsure of its origin). We behave according to patterns rather than assessing what we need or want. The key to this exercise is to be thoughtful about what we do and what we don't do.

While this is an exercise that will spark your thinking about living intentionally, this is just the beginning. Living intentionally is a lifelong process, which gets easier the more we do it, but it requires us to continually be aware of what facilitates being our best selves.

Take time to set your intentions. This is a good exercise to do at the beginning of the year, the month, the week, even the day. Setting your intentions is about living authentically, not about getting your to-do list accomplished. (However, mastering our to-do list may help us live intentionally.) How do you want to show up today, this week, this month? How do you want to intentionally reclaim being a bitch? Speaking up when you feel the fear of letting your thoughts be known?

How do you want to intentionally focus on self-care, changing your health holistically?

Filling your vase

Sometimes setting intentions means being mindful of how we want to act. For example, I want to be respectful toward all people I encounter, whether it be through email, telephone, or in person. That is very different than saying at the end of the day that I didn't mean to be disrespectful.

Setting the positive intention filters our interactions towards that intention and allows our subconscious to begin working.

This parable illustrates the importance of setting these intentions. Origin – unknown, message – timeless.

A professor stood before his class with a large empty vase and several large rocks, a jar of pebbles, a bucket of sand, and a pitcher of water. He filled the vase to the top with the large rocks and asked his students if the vase was full. The students confirmed that vase was full.

He then added the pebbles to the vase, and shook the vase to let the pebbles settle among the larger rocks. Then he asked again, "Is the vase full now?" The students again agreed the vase was full, but they are now beginning to see a pattern (because students are very smart!).

The professor then poured sand into the vase, with the sand settling between the pebbles. The students then agreed the vase was completely full. The professor then poured the water into the vase, such that the water permeated the sand and the vase was full.

The professor explained that the vase represents your life. The larger rocks represent the things that mean the most to you in your life (family, health, purpose). If you could only have these rocks in your vase, then your life would be meaningful. The pebbles symbolize those things in your life that matter (hobbies, job, friends) but are not critical for you to have a meaningful life. These things often come and go, and are not essential to your overall well-being.

The sand stands for the things that maintain your current life, but you could change your priorities and your life would have meaning without them.in your life, such as maintaining or obtaining possessions, running errands.

The water, then, symbolizes the things in your life that are likely only done to waste time or get small tasks accomplished, such as Netflix, or social media (!).

If you fill your vase with water or sand first, you will not have room for rocks or pebbles. This holds true with the things you let into your life. If you spend most of your time on the small and insignificant things, you will run out of room for the things that are important to you. Please note – these categories are self-defined, so one person's water may be another person's rock. Each of us needs to choose how to intentionally fill our vase.

Pause: Living Intentionally

In order to live a more intentional life, you must define the components, and pay attention to the "rocks," the things that will matter in the long term. The rocks are your priorities, while the other things in your life are represented by pebbles, sand, and water. In order to stay productive and efficient in your personal and professional life, five rocks is likely the most you can have in your vase at one time. We may say our family is a rock, but we may not act that way, putting the pebbles in first. If you fill your vase with pebbles first, there is no room left for your rocks.

Exercise: Identify your rocks. How, specifically, can you set aside the time you need to focus on them today, this week, this month, this year? Do you need to take out some of your pebbles, sand, and water to allow space for your rocks? You may want to buy yourself a vase, gather some rocks, grab some pebbles and sand and create a visual cue to remind you to focus on your priorities, to live with intention.

Work on your rocks first. Put them on your to-do list. Make time for them so you are intentionally living the life you want.

Chapter 6: The Empowered Inner Bitch

We have focused on finding and excavating your inner bitch. This section contains tools and exercises to help nurture and develop your inner bitch. Incorporating intentional practice will keep you consciously aware of what your inner bitch wants and needs.

The Responsibility Bulls-Eye

We all have qualities or strengths that make us unique, qualities we draw upon regularly. Understanding our strengths allows us to build on what we do well, allowing our inner bitch to flourish. It also highlights areas of growth, places we may want to dampen some of our strengths if we are overusing them or bolster some of our less used qualities into strengths.

A few years back I attended a women's leadership program, the Women's Executive Leadership Program[12] for which the prep work included taking the Strength Finders[13] assessment, a tool that ranks you on 34 strengths. The facilitator casually explained our strengths are innate, which led me down a path of discovery because I disagreed.

None of this could be right, I thought. I did not innately have the strengths the assessment illuminated. Particularly because I was not very happy with them. Sure, some of them were okay. I knew I was an "input," one who seeks and gathers information. You could tell by my overflowing book shelves. And I knew I was a "relator," one who values one on one relationships and getting to know people individually. But I rejected the "responsibility" strength as inherent and innate. I knew I felt great responsibility but if it is innate, then there is less flexibility and little opportunity for change. That is a strength I desperately wanted to put to the side and ignore. So what did I do? I used my "intellection" (one who uses intellectual abilities to solve problems), my "achiever" (one who seeks to achieve), and my "input" to do some research. I was determined to figure this out.

Turns out the facilitator was wrong and also a little right. Our strengths are a **product** of our talents plus the investment into that talent. Ah ha! That was the answer for me. I could look back on my life and see the significant and frequent investment into all of my strengths. I received positive reinforcement repeatedly for my responsibility strength. Who doesn't want to be around someone who will be responsible for making sure everything is going well, making sure things run smoothly and are under control? I see my responsibility strength as a blessing and a curse. Yes, it has gotten me far, and it is primarily what I do for my career. I take responsibility for making sure things get done. However, many times, I overused this strength. I took on feelings of responsibility for things over which I had no control, and I internalized these feelings, which ultimately affected my sleep and well-being.

My inner bitch was hiding under a blanket of responsibility. I had ignored her as she reminded me that certain things were not my responsibility. As a child, I felt responsible for my parents' happiness and well-being. Not your responsibility, my inner bitch said. But I ignored her. And over time, she stopped trying. Until I started excavating her. While I still have the tendency to feel responsible for everything, including the weather when people are visiting, I hear my inner bitch reminding me that I am not responsible. I can only do what I can do to facilitate success and then I have to let go. Everyone has his/her own free will. I do not have control of everything.

I decided at that time that I was going to invest in some of the other strengths, slowly, intentionally. I was going to work on lessening the achiever and the responsibility strengths. They are so incredibly strong that minimizing them slightly will be of little negative and much positive consequence. My input strength is insatiable and I am happy to feed it. I love reading, learning, inputting. I can see this in my dad as well. He spends hours collecting, cataloguing, and storing information in case he someday needs it, much to my mom's chagrin. But I love this strength of his – it keeps him engaged and vital. And I love that about mine as well.

But responsibility? Could do with a little less of that. I have noticed that my journal entries over time are strikingly similar in this regard. To be kind to myself, it is challenging as a mother in our society to not feel responsible. Freud did a number on women years ago – blaming moms for just about everything, and the blame was easy to perpetuate. We all know it is common to see behaviors in children and blame the mom for not molding the child in a different way. We also have been victim of our children holding us responsible for various things, many of which we could not possibly be responsible for, including not having the favorite pair of jeans washed and ready to wear even though they are hiding in the deep, dark crevices under the bed. Some of us are better at letting this roll off our backs. Me? Nope. I have a responsibility bulls-eye on my forehead. Responsibility has been a driving factor in my life. I look at my life plan and see my responsibility strength like a flashing neon sign.

Responsible! Responsible! You are responsible! Do the responsible thing!

I can also view my life path with my other strengths in mind. The relator strength has brought me here. I want to coach people to reach their potential personally and professionally. I want to help people think about whether their stories still fit. I want to relate to people on multiple levels. It allows me to succeed professionally. Being able to speak to all kinds of people makes it easier to connect and work with them. My inner bitch wants me to celebrate my strengths and recognize that my unique combination of qualities makes me who I am. She wants me to utilize those strengths to maximize my and others' potential. She also wants me to recognize when I am overusing those strengths, to my own or others' detriment, and to strive for balance.

I know changing my thoughts can change my life. I want to focus on the strengths I like. I am proud of being a relator, of being able to talk to people comfortably, making them feel like the most important person in the room. I am an achiever, always have been. And input, well, collecting knowledge and information is awesome. There is so much to learn! I think I need new bookshelves, though.

Pause: Strengths and Weaknesses

There are multiple ways to figure out your strengths. You can take an assessment like Strength Finders[13], which offers you two versions – one for about $20 which provides you with your top 5 strengths and the other for about $50 which ranks you on all 34 strengths. The more extensive version allowed me to see the strengths that I don't often exercise. For example, woo (the ability to win others over) is one of my least used strengths. When I meet someone who has woo, I know it. And I want it. I have contemplated ways to increase the strengths I don't often use, and it means getting out of my comfort zone. Some I am fine not nurturing. But – woo? Who doesn't want more woo? To me that means being in situations where I use charisma to encourage others to follow my ideas. The hard part is that my relator skill is strong – and then I naturally go to the more intellectual approach to express myself. Oh well, woo may be part of my top 30 someday.

The second approach to finding your strengths is to ask others. Find five or ten people who know you well and who you trust to be honest with you. Ask them what they think your strengths are. You can also give them some time to think about it, but many will be able to list them for you right away. If you are a visual person, create a mind map of people's answers. If you are analytical like me, you can create a spreadsheet of responses.

The third way is quite revealing about how we think of ourselves. You will need some paper, a pen, and a timer. Set the timer for 2 minutes and list as many of your weaknesses or 'areas of growth' that you can. Then put that piece of paper away and get a fresh one. Now set the timer for 4 minutes. List as many strengths as you can. Be thoughtful and come up with as many as you can. Do this now. Seriously. Ready? Go!

How did you do? Many of us find that we have no trouble listing weaknesses. They come easily to us. The strengths are harder. We have been taught over the years to be humble and not blow our own horn. Blow away! Celebrate your strengths. Magnify them. Dance over them. Your strengths are what make you uniquely you. Use our energy wisely and know when to delegate the tasks we are weaker on to others who have strengths in that area. I know that I am not going to shine with woo, so if I think I am going to need woo in a situation (and who doesn't, really?) then I bring along my woo-y friends or colleagues. But after they woo a person, I can step in and relate to her, give her the information she wants, and be the one responsible for following through. Yes, you heard me. I claimed my responsibility strength. Denying it is no longer an option. Minimizing it is, however.

Be creative with these exercises. Baking, writing, painting, singing – all can be strengths. Empathy, vision setting, attention to detail. Strengths can be many things and these three exercises tap into different kinds of strengths. At the very least, do the last two – they are free and quick. And will be quite informative for you.

Affirmations (aka Life Statements)

Our thoughts create our emotions, which create our beliefs, which create our actions, which create our habits, which create our lives. Changing our thoughts, then, can ultimately change our lives. Seems impossible that something we can't even see, of which we are often unaware, has such power. But it's true. What we focus on grows in our lives. If you spend your days looking for people being snippy or irritable, you will find them. If you are continually looking for good, you will find it. If you believe you are shy, you will act that way. If you believe your inner bitch is unburied and thriving, you will be empowered, feel freer to say what you need in a way others can hear it, and live a more fulfilled life. I have been writing affirmations for a solid two years. I began with the idea that – well, if it doesn't work, it only takes minutes a day, and I am empowered through the action. No real loss. After these two years, I am convinced it works.

What are affirmations? Great question. Affirmations are positive statements about yourself or your life. I prefer to call mine life statements because it is less about me as a person and more about what I am bringing into my life. Both are valuable; both are important; both work. My list contains both. When I think of traditional affirmations, I think of statements like, "I am strong, healthy, and pain-free." This statement is on my list. Also, "I am balanced and centered." On my list. And I take another approach as well. I write statements of belief about what I want to come into my life.

While I believe that manifestation works, that there are realms of our lives that we know very little about, I think there are multiple logical reasons to accompany the more woo-woo idea that the universe brings you what you need. I believe that everything we want and need is waiting for us – though it may not look exactly the way we think it will. Sometimes, however, it looks exactly the way we want – and it can be awe-inspiring. Note: depending on your religious and spiritual beliefs, some may prefer to refer to this as God, some may say it is the universe, some may say it's karma. The point is not what you call it, it's what you believe.

I started this practice in January, 2017, while on a snowmobiling trip to Wyoming.

******

This trip is worth a short aside. Approximately two years prior to the trip, a friend suggested a snowmobiling trip to Yellowstone. I laughed, literally, out loud. People! I grew up in Hawaii. I hate being cold. Spending three days zooming around on a snowmobile (in January! In Wyoming!) was definitely NOT my idea of a vacation. That sounded horrid.

Fast forward a year. Our friend suggested it again – in the middle of summer. Brian seemed genuinely interested. And I had begun working at consciously stepping out of my comfort zone. Here it was – the optimal opportunity to step into my desire for a lack of comfort. Completely. No toe-dipping here. This was diving into the deep end of the ice bath. So, I agreed. And then I thought, 'OMG. What have I done?' Luckily (not), I had five months to prepare myself (i.e., dread the trip). We made our hotel reservations, got our flights, arranged for dog-sledding and snow-shoeing expeditions (because snowmobiling was simply not enough).

A few weeks before the trip, our friend mentioned some of the gear they had purchased – snow goggles, long underwear, balaclavas, and warm gloves. We went into panic mode. We hadn't been thinking about preparing! We are only a few weeks away, and we didn't have anything like that. We were able to find everything but the snow goggles. Great. We were going to have frozen eyeballs and frostbitten noses. But fortunately, our friends (3 hours south of us) were able to find them for us.

Two weeks before the trip, we had a winter event in Durham. For those of you who reside to the north of North Carolina, let me explain. Winter in the south is nothing like winter in the north. After spending six years in Pennsylvania, I thought winter meant snow, snow plows, snow shovels, and piles of dirty snow on the side of the road. In North Carolina it means snow melting and then refreezing into a slippery, slidy mess. Our few inches of snow melts slightly, freezes into an impassable sheet of ice, and the cycle continues for as long as it takes for the daytime sun to melt the mess completely. During this particular winter event, we had quite a bit of ice on the roads. I remember thinking – man, I've done it now. I can't believe I agreed to spend a week in Wyoming in winter, let alone go on a snowmobile for three days! But the deed was done – our flight was in fewer days than the number of fingers on my hands. Chin up, buttercup! Might as well embrace my opportunity to step out (way out) of my comfort zone.

The moment we flew into the Jackson Hole airport, I was stunned by the beauty of the mountains, the snow, and the wide expanse of amazing-ness. Truly, this was the most awe-inspiring trip I have ever taken. Stepping out of my comfort zone literally changed my life. It put me in a zone that allowed me to see so many things clearly. I took a risk and saw a whole side of the world, and myself, that I might not have encountered. Maybe it was the clear air, maybe it was the outrageous cold (record-breaking cold and snow that

January – which says a lot considering we were in WYOMING!), maybe it was taking a risk to get out of my comfort zone, or maybe it was getting out of my routine and stepping into the arena of my life. Maybe it was all of it combined. I am grateful my inner bitch pushed me into the icy waters.

******

I do not remember what inspired me to start writing life statements. I read a lot and sometimes I experience source amnesia – not remembering where I read something. I find that to be true especially when I read on my Kindle. Without seeing the actual book cover, holding it in my hands, I don't have the memory triggers available for me. Anyway – it was not the first time that I had read about affirmations but I had previously dismissed them, because my image of standing in front of the mirror, telling myself how wonderful I am did not resonate with me. I knew instinctively that I was not going to keep that habit going. But writing them and making them forward thinking? That I could do. I had read amazing stories of people making vision boards, putting them away for years, and then upon unearthing them, discovering that their visions had come true. I thought – I want in on that! I thought – well, what's the harm if it doesn't work? Sounds reasonable to me.

My scientific mind was intrigued by the evidence. My responsible mind was comforted by the fact that it didn't take much time. My idealistic mind was all in. So I began. I have written them nearly every day since. I try not to be legalistic about anything I do. If I don't get to them one day, that is okay. I already had a solid morning routine. This was easy to add. And it was fun. I enjoyed spending time thinking about what I wanted to bring into my life.

Being on a trip, thinking about preparations (or lack thereof) for the trip, made me contrast that preparation for my life. I also thought long and hard about how we hadn't really prepared for the trip, until we were prodded by our friends. Those thoughts swirled in my head. I wanted to spend at least as much time planning my life as I would for a vacation. I wanted to be sure I prepared in whatever ways I could – thinking about where I want to go, being clear on my direction, acquiring the provisions and tools I need. The idea of affirmations is that we are not responsible for the how, only the what. The how will happen. Our job is to put the idea out to the universe. For me, this meant writing it daily.

The view on manifesting is that what we put out to the universe, we receive. So we want to do it thoughtfully. Rather than saying what we don't want, we want to say what we do want. Putting the negative out there is more likely to bring the negative back to us. In other words, if I were a fashion model about to walk the runway, I would not want to say, "I am not going to fall on the runway." Rather, I would say, "I am going to walk down that runway like I own it." Focusing on the negative, even if it is disguised as a positive, will bring the negative. Think about what you want, not what you don't want.

What we think we become. Our thoughts truly do direct our actions, which become our habits, which ultimately guide our lives. This is a calculated way to practice changing our lives through changing our thoughts. Seems a bit odd to talk about calculated ways to bring manifestation into our lives, but it is important to recognize that this is not all woo-woo. This is neuroscience. I believe in systems, I believe in routine, I believe in science. And now I believe in affirmations.

But, honestly, I didn't like the name. It still brought up images of me smiling at myself in the mirror, telling myself "You rock!" or "You are awesome!" That didn't suit me. It may suit others perfectly, and that is great. There are as many ways to implement these practices as there are people. I needed to change the name, for myself, to life statements - things I believe I will have in my life. And I am stepping into that belief, just like I stepped into my dis-comfort zone and found it to be one of the most amazing experiences in my life. Life-changing.

My very first life statement said "I will thrive in my beach house, where I will write, read, and grow." January, 2017, in Jackson Hole, Wyoming. We closed on our beach house in North Carolina in December, 2017. The universe delivered. But this is when my scientist brain also comes into play. Writing these statements brings them to my consciousness every day. I take action toward those life statements, as I step into the belief. I believe it is the synchrony between the universe working on my behalf, my taking steps toward changing my thoughts, beliefs, actions, habits, and my recognizing the opportunities in front of me.

I believe this is immensely powerful – when I am writing these life statements every day, I am looking at life through that lens. I am attracting, recognizing, and remaining open to opportunity that flows to me. I want to see the opportunity in front of me. And I am primed to do so because I am clear about what I want in my life. I have stepped into some opportunities that have blossomed and some that have not. But I may not have recognized the opportunity if I hadn't been primed. I am more likely to think about, talk about, and act on my life statements. When I talk about them, others hear my ideas, they make connections to things going on in their lives, including people they know, and serendipity happens.

Back to the beach house. How that happened can be nothing less than the universe at play, showing me – yes, I will bring you what you want. Just believe. And pay attention – see what is going on around you. Live life fully, not in a daze. Get off the treadmill. Or at least look around while you are on it.

We safely made it back from our snowmobiling trip. I had one task that I was supposed to do sometime in the spring – but I kept putting it off. I was supposed to reserve a friend's beach house on the Outer Banks of North Carolina for the first week in August so my daughter, Amanda, and I could spend some time at the beach. Yep. By the time I got around to it, the house was booked. So I had to come up with plan B. Amanda took the lead and found a place for a few days in Calabash, NC. Not quite the same – definitely not walking distance to the beach, but we were certain we would have a grand time anyway.

Off we went. Amanda and I walked miles on the various beaches. On one of our walks, I casually said to Amanda, "Someday we are going to own a beach house." She stopped walking, turned to me, and said, "When are you going to live your dream, Mom? You keep making my dreams come true. Don't you think it's time you do the same for yours?" I do not know why it took my then 20-year-old daughter to jolt me into reality. But I am grateful.

On Labor Day weekend, Brian and I went down to look at houses. I walked many miles during our house-hunting journeys. The beach was sprinkled with pieces of sand dollars. Although I had grown up in Hawaii, I had never seen a whole sand dollar on the beach. I declared that finding a whole sand dollar would be my sign that it was time to buy a beach house. A challenge to the universe? Yes. I was challenging the universe with my life statement about thriving in a beach house AND having to find a whole sand dollar. And I was likely subconsciously protecting myself from taking this big step. But the universe delivered. In a big way.

It took us several weeks of driving to the beach, but I found the house I liked in November. And the one I liked is related to another of my life statements. I wanted to start having retreats for women who wanted to think about their lives. To find or recharge their inner bitch. I would walk into every house and envision my retreat guests in the house. I was embodying two of my life statements at one time. And that is how I believe it works. It is the magical combination of the universe providing opportunity and serendipity, and my looking through the lens of possibility, believing that we are living in a world of abundance and that I will receive what I put out there.

But I hadn't found my sand dollar yet, so I was not ready to make my move. Silly me. I went for a walk the morning after seeing the house for the first time, one hour before my appointment to see it the second time. As I was walking off the beach at the end of my walk, a whole sand dollar peered up at me. There was my sign.

Incredible. I looked at the house the second time and knew that this was the one. And the universe made sure I understood. After looking at the house the second time, I went back to the beach to contemplate the decision. It was low tide, and I was shocked to see sand dollars everywhere. In the knee-deep water, 150 more sand dollars were waiting for me. CRAZY! I stopped picking them up after about an

206

hour – I could have gathered more. But I had my sign(s). And now I have my beach house.

Two years after starting writing my life statements, I have realized some of them. I have removed some after I decided they weren't really what I wanted and added others. I have added statements of abundance in health, fitness, sleep, finances, and career. I have a statement that I will write this book by the end of the year.

This is a great example of how the combination of my own agency and my belief in the universe conspire together to make my life statements come true. I had been writing this statement since March 2018. At that time, 2018 seemed endless. In October of 2018, I realized I better get my act together if I were going to write this book in 2018. So I began to sit down to write every day. I wrote from 4 am to 7 am on weekdays and longer on weekends. I added additional life statements – "I write effortlessly and prolifically," and "I write meaningful books that add value to people's lives." AND I sat my butt down every day, e-v-e-r-y d-a-y to write. I created a graphic of the book cover, with New York Times bestseller plastered across the top (might as well put it in the universe). I finished the book in February 2019. I didn't make my 2018 deadline, but having the date in my statement made me start writing.

Believe, step into, and act. Jim Carey[14] has a great story about how he manifested abundance in his life. At the beginning of his career, he would visualize the things he wanted in his career, including directors liking his work. Hewrote himself a check for ten million dollars for acting services rendered, dated a few years forward. He carried it in his wallet, believing he would be rich and famous one day. He added his own agency by saying although he believed the universe was going to make him a great actor, bringing him multiple opportunities, he would still drive himself to the auditions. Right before the check date, he found out he was going to make ten million dollars for a movie. Manifestation plus personal agency – the secret sauce.

The combination of journaling and life statements is powerful; it is the full expression of the inner bitch. Sometimes it takes hindsight to see the connections between the opportunities and the life statement. Sometimes I'll be talking with someone, and the conversation will take a new twist, down the path of one of my life statements, and things begin to happen. It feels like all paths led there – even though the signposts were not in full view.

Pause: Life Statements

There are many ways to have a life statement or affirmation practice. I have a journal dedicated to my life statements, so I have a collection of statements, written day after day. Flipping through this journal is a powerful indication of the power of intention and manifestation. I love to look back over the days, weeks, months to see what is no longer there – and what remains. For me, it's a powerful statement of the gifts I have given myself – time, nurturing, belief, power.

But you can put them in your regular journal as well, as an addition to your daily journal entry. You can say your affirmations out loud every day and not write them at all. You can say them while looking in a mirror. Try a few different approaches and see what feels right for you.

However you approach it, the key is to do the affirmations/life statements daily. Don't be inflexible, though. If you miss a day, pick it up the next day, or do it at a different time that day. I encourage you to keep this practice up for at least three months, preferably six months or more, to allow time for it to work.

Find a time every day that you will write your life statements. With any habit you are trying to create, you are more likely to be successful if you anchor the activity to another habit. For example, I added my life statement writing to my journal writing, first thing in the morning, both anchored to my first cup of coffee. I like to start my day with my life statements because they offer me the lens through which I see the activities of my day. Some, however, may find the evening is a good time for them. Some say that writing the affirmations at night before bed allows their brain to work on them while sleeping, unleashing the power of the subconscious. Regularity is more important than timing. Find the time that works for you.

Be specific and clear in your statements. Add a time frame around them as well, when appropriate. "I will write FYIB by the end of the year." This time frame added accountability, making me put my butt in the chair. The universe can only do so much – I have to grab either a pen or a keyboard so the book can flow through my fingers. Many recommend adding the phrase, "or something better" to the end of each statement. This acknowledges that there may be something better than our limited minds could come fathom.

You may not receive in the exact form you anticipate. Sometimes things happen in a way that is different but better than you could have imagined. Do not dwell on what you don't want. Reframe those statements into positive ones – "I will not be afraid" becomes "I will be brave." "I won't run out of money" becomes "I will be able to pay my bills easily, with money leftover." This is an excellent opportunity to create life statements that rewrite your childhood stories.

I'm excited for you – I believe this is one of the most powerful things you can do. Start by considering what you want in life, either in the near future or in the long-term. How do you want to approach your days? For example, I have a combination of short- and long-term statements. I write "I prioritize myself in all things" as a reminder to put my oxygen mask on first, to think about what all decisions mean for me. This does not mean that I make all decisions only with regard to me, but it does mean that I am consciously choosing what is best, taking myself into consideration. I also have statements about long-term financial security. I used to have statements about living near my grandchildren, loving life with them. But then I thought I better remove those statements for now. I didn't want the universe to be confused and send me grandchildren too soon.

My statements change occasionally, but overall I write the same things every day. When something comes to fruition, it gets removed or altered. For example, last year I wrote, "I pilot my *Sol Searching* retreat this year." When I piloted the retreat, I changed the life statement to "I run 4^+ successful retreats per year." Be flexible with yourself and have fun. When something no longer feels right, remove it. You can always put it back.

Be forewarned – I completely believe this works, so be prepared for the wonderful things that you are going to be bringing into your life. I have had to take a step back every once in a while to say – whoa! I need a pause. But this has helped me refine my life statements. For example, if one of my life statements is that my retreat business takes off beyond my wildest dreams, the side effect of that is that it also takes more time and requires more of me, or at least requires a re-visioning. Be thoughtful about what you write. And remember that your own agency and action is part of the equation. I couldn't get my book written if I didn't sit down to do it. But, I also didn't worry about the final product when I sat down. I just wrote. Prolifically and abundantly, remaining unattached to the outcome during the process. When I began to think about the big picture, when I began to worry about how I was going to put all the pieces together, I became paralyzed into inaction. So I just went back to sitting my butt down, doing my part and letting the universe do hers. And I listened to my inner bitch. She guided me the whole way.

My Inner Bitch Expressing Herself

I started writing in a journal in the fall of 1995, when Brayton and Ben were 2 ½ years and five months old, respectively. For the next 24 years, I have written in the morning – sometimes regularly, sometimes with big gaps, chronicling my challenges (many) and triumphs (few). Upon rereading these journals, I am struck by a few things.

First, many of my struggles were recurring. Perhaps not occurring in exactly the same way, but reappearing with amazing regularity. My inner bitch was trying to tell me something along the way. Second, I spent much more time talking about what I did poorly than what I did well. I was really hard on myself. Again and again. A constant barrage of – "You should have spoken more gently to your defiant toddler. You should spend more time sitting on the floor playing with them. You should not hesitate to pick up your two-year-old for the twelfth time in a day to carry him up the stairs, because, you know, he is going to grow up and he won't want you doing that anymore."

Well, okay, that is true. My 24-year-old son definitely does not want me to carry him up the stairs anymore. And it is also true that we need to remember that those early days flow swiftly. But when this little one was two, I also had a four-year-old and an infant. I had already carried that sweet boy up the stairs nearly a dozen times that day. In my journal, I ask myself, "Why not pick him up and give him the love and reassurance he is asking for? He will be grown soon enough." Oh, the mom guilt. The eagerness to take care of everyone else and stifle the inner bitch that gently says to me – "Enough. You have done enough. You are mom enough." When I look back on my parenting of my small children, I remember distinctly embracing the moments, the small moments that I knew were fleeting. I made career choices that allowed me to be at home most of the time with them – deciding to forego career advancement after 10 years of college and graduate work and three years of a post-doctoral fellowship. And I did it willingly. But, for God's sake, give myself a break! A mom absolutely needs to put on her oxygen mask first, especially if she is going to be carrying a two-year-old up the stairs eleven times in a day.

My noisy roommate was much louder and more talkative than my inner bitch. The roommate pointed out my frustration, my not-so-perfect parenting, my tendency toward a house filled with piles of projects and dirty laundry. I wrote in my journals to work through difficult times – so it is not surprising that the journals are filled with challenges. However, I am also aware that what I had written was the norm – I was quick to judge and hold myself to extreme standards. At one point in time, I was homeschooling, teaching at an elite university, parenting three children under five, managing my roles as a wife and home keeper, and watching other people's children as well to bring in extra income and provide a much needed service for other moms working outside the home. Kudos to me! That is incredible.

Occasionally I wrote about how tired I was (understandable) but mostly I wrote about how I was not doing it all well enough or even doing enough. I baked continuously, almost maniacally sometimes, as if I were trying to prove my worth through delicious deliverables. What was I trying to prove and to whom? Well, that is actually fairly simple. I **was** trying to prove my worth. I **was** trying to prove to society that I wasn't wasting my life by not pursuing a full-time career. I was very busy justifying my days – and when I look back 20 years later, it was the energy spent justifying,

214

worrying about what others thought about the choices I made, which was the waste. If only we were kinder and gentler to each other and ourselves in our society. If only we didn't have a prescribed particular path. If only I was braver and had allowed my inner bitch to scream from the rooftop – "I am enough! I am doing enough! My choices are valid! I am a contributing member of society even if I decide not to pursue full time employment after spending umpteen years preparing for it."

My inner bitch wanted me to be home with the kids and for the kids to be home with me. I wanted to be there. She tells me this repeatedly throughout the first several years of journal writing. I would swirl about job offers, proposals to write, tasks that needed to be done. I would decide, reconsider, and decide again about sending our oldest to preschool. And then I would continue to ruminate about it, not finding peace in my decision. I couldn't easily listen to my inner bitch, as much as I wanted to, because I had done such a good job silencing her, stuffing her down, having my noisy roommate out speak her. But she is there – in those pages. Clearly.

Then the next paragraph takes me down the spiral again – but what if? What if he doesn't get into a good college because I don't send him to preschool? Seriously, real fears. What if they are behind in their learning compared to other five-year-olds? What if they don't learn to stand in line and otherwise be good citizens? What if we can't make it without two salaries? What if I never work again and have completely wasted my PhD and those six years of graduate education? If only we had….The "what if's" and "if only's" put me in a swirl. My inner bitch knew what to do, but I was afraid to be resolute about those decisions. Afraid to say –

"This is what I believe, and we will work it out. There is more than one path in life, and I want to take the one less traveled. I hear it is beautiful."

The process of writing in the journals was and continues to be cathartic for me. As evidenced in the journals, I worked through my decisions, challenges, and struggles. I also wrote down the funny things the kids said or did because I knew I wouldn't remember them as time passed. And the observations I made about the kids as they were growing up are so special to me now.

Simply the physical process of writing helps me in many ways. It helps me get the swirl out of my head, releasing the hold it has on my mind. Granted, sometimes I have to write about it for days (and sometimes revisit it over the years, even decades), but knowing it is captured somewhere allows my mind to rest. Also, giving myself the space and time to focus on myself was and is an important form of self-care. The journal writing itself was a manifestation of my inner bitch. To take care of myself, spend time in thought and meditation. And to get glimpses of the inner bitch – what she thought, what she needed.

Reading the journals also has provided me with perspective. Sometimes the decisions I spent hours and days focusing on are small in hindsight. And the energy I spent worrying about what others thought held me hostage in many situations. Reading these things in my own words and my own handwriting acts like a beacon for moving forward. The decisions that could have gone either way – when I could argue in my own head for either side or even multiple sides. Everything turns out okay – even when there were consequences to my decisions. I learned from them, I made the best decision I could, given what I knew at the time. Mostly I am grateful for the decisions I made. For example,

I turned down several jobs when my second child was an infant, making the conscious choice to step out of the full-time workforce so I could be with our children. I clearly delineated the choices – I was giving up financial rewards and gaining time and memories with our children. And I don't regret it for a second. Perhaps our current net worth would be higher if I had taken one of those jobs, but the riches we gained from my being at home far surpass any possible financial gain.

Giving my inner bitch her voice

Keeping a journal gave my inner bitch the platform she needed to express herself. I didn't always listen, and often my noisy roommate was louder than she was. But over time, the messages my inner bitch gave me were the threads that offered insight into who I was at my core. The journals gave me a space and venue for writing down my deepest fears, enabling me to see my emotions and fears wouldn't make me self-implode. I could express them and be okay. I could then let them sit. I could pause in the knowing that I had been honest with myself and that I had been heard. And then, when the time was right, I could decide if I wanted to act. Through the consistency of journal writing, I was able to uncover my true self. I could be vulnerable in a safe way. Author and shame researcher Brené Brown[15] talks about deliberately choosing who is privileged enough to receive your vulnerability. I was giving myself the privilege of being vulnerable to myself. And a privilege it truly is.

Journaling gave me the mechanism with which to work on problem solving. There are a fair number of pros and cons lists in my journals. Although I don't think that is the most effective method for solving problems, the process allowed me to enumerate the many things I was thinking. I needed to get the swirl out of my head. Putting it on paper released my hold on it, and gave me back the energy the constant swirl was taking. Journal writing also triggered gratitude for me. Many a morning were spent enumerating how many wonderful things I had in my life. And for that, I am grateful.

The gift of journaling

Journaling is a bit like budgeting. It can be very helpful but when people think about it, it seems overwhelming and hard to get started. Kind of funny that I make this analogy, because I don't budget. But I do journal. My very first journal entry was a bit awkward, because I can tell I felt like I had to say something profound at the launch of this process. Who knew at that time, 24 years ago, that I would keep it up? I wanted to but I had a 2-year-old and an infant. How the heck was I going to write in a journal? I am so glad I did. My dedication to it waned and flowed, but to have those 24 years of my life chronicled – wow. Truly I feel like it is one of the greatest gifts I have given myself. Ever. Better than a Tiffany box. One of my students claimed the box from Tiffany's was a gift in itself because of the beautiful color and ribbon. The box is a beautiful container for what is inside. Just like us. Everything inside us is special, to be cherished.

Journaling – it is both an immediate and a long-term gift. The process of journaling is cathartic. Sitting down, taking the time for just me feels like a luxury. And I deserve the luxury. Ironically, this is one of the reasons women give me for not journaling. "I don't have time." I didn't have time not to journal. It is exhausting trying to remember everything, to continually work through decisions or conflicts in my head. If I can sit and even bullet out my thoughts, I can rest, knowing I can return to it. My journal is sitting there waiting for me. It is holding my debate.

The key, and I wasn't always good at this, was to remember that I was only writing for me, for the moment. The journals are a gift of time, for sure. But the process is about capturing the moment, working through questions, doubts, insecurities. The journal was a way to jot down the funny things the kids said or did. If I sat down, just for the moment and just for me, I knew I could write anything or nothing. It could be gibberish, and it often was, because it was the process of writing I was seeking, not the product. My physical journals are mostly different. In the past few years, I have found my journal of choice (by Gallery Leather[16]), a lined large journal. I love the feel of the paper and the cover. I feel luxurious writing in it. And that is the point. It is a luxury to take the time to write in a journal. I am worth it. It is a luxury to buy a higher end journal, and I am worth it. The daily investment, both in time and in money, is miniscule when put in perspective. But I have used many different things as journals, partially because I was searching for what worked best and partially because I didn't have time when the kids were younger to be on a search for the perfect journal.

I love starting a new journal, and I love ending a journal. I often meditate on the blank pages – thinking about how I will be filling them. What will go in there? What will the next few months, or years hold? I never know how long a journal will last. It depends. It depends on how many distractions I have. While writing this book, my journal sat quietly waiting. I used it more often during this time period to plan upcoming retreats, ideas for workshops, business plans. My journal is a lot like those friends who you know are there, even when you don't see them often. Friends with whom you could have coffee and pick up where you left off. They are comfortable, and they love you no matter what.

When I go back and read the journals from the past, many themes pop out at me, anxieties that resurface again and again, ever-present insecurities, my tendency toward busyness. But what I also see, which at the time would have surprised me, is how tender my heart was, how vulnerable I was, how I was trying so hard and yet being so very hard on myself. When I look back at 30-year-old Pam, 35-year-old Pam, 40-year-old Pam, 45-year-old Pam, and even 50-year-old Pam, I think –

"Wow, you are so special. Look within. Your inner bitch is telling you something. Listen. You are worthy. You do not need to keep striving. You do not need to prove yourself. You do not need to be all things to all people. In fact, you do not need to be all things to the people you love. You just need to be you. There is no one else who can do that. People see more than the wrinkles under your eyes, which is all you focus on sometimes. People don't judge you on the jiggly part under your arms. Well, maybe some do, but truly you don't care about them. Remember what Jessie J says in her song, Masterpiece – 'Those who mind don't matter and those who matter don't mind.'"

I would also tell those Pams – celebrate. Take the time to breathe. Pause. Take a step back. Step off the treadmill. Be gentle with yourself. Trust your inner bitch. Looking back, I can see the times I swayed like a weak tree in the wind – how to be a good mom, how to be a good homeschool teacher, how to be a good wife, how to be good at so many different roles. And during those times, I used my input and responsibility strengths to gather information, to take on the task at hand, to learn the best way possible. But I didn't listen to myself well enough. I had the answers. I knew what I wanted. I didn't trust myself. But all of that led me here. And I am happy here.

I am proud of myself – I am so very proud of myself for giving myself the time to journal. To exercise. To read. I held that time as sacred. I am proud of that. I am a morning person. I taught our oldest at a very young age how to read a clock. He would wake up way before the sun to start his, and my, day. So I taught him what 7:00 looked like on a digital clock. He was not allowed to come downstairs until 7. That allowed me my time – to journal, read, be. Journaling had the side effect of allowing me to be a better mom because I had started the day doing something just for me. I worked through some of my challenges. I knew they were written in the journal, waiting for me; I didn't need to perseverate about them.

Pause: Just Do It

Commit to journaling in some form for a month. I am by nature a writer. Writing is how I work through my thoughts, how I express myself. Not everyone likes to write. How to journal is up for debate. I prefer hand written journals. I love the feeling of the pen on paper. I like to flip through actual pages to see what I have written. Not even specifics about what I have written, but seeing my words, my handwriting on the pages makes me feel like I have been taking care of myself. Others prefer to journal on the computer, typing their words. I can appreciate the value of having electronic journals. Themes in 20+ paper journals are hard to search and analyze.

For me, the process of writing with pen and paper is critical. For the same reason I prefer to take handwritten notes in meetings, I need to write my journals in pen. My hand, connected to the pen, creating my handwriting, is the tool for my thoughts to form. I am certainly less likely to do a quick "let's see what the weather will be" or "I wonder if there is something I need to buy from somewhere" rabbit trail if I am using a paper journal than if I am sitting with my laptop on my lap. I know – because several boxes have arrived at my doorstep throughout the process of writing this book on my laptop.

This is your journal. You can do it anyway you like. You can try it multiple ways. I would suggest that you try the handwritten journal first, knowing that I am admittedly biased. There is something about buying a journal that appeals to your inner bitch – one that says "please fill me." There is wonder in moving your hands over the blank pages. And there is even more wonder in moving your hands over the filled pages. It is a physical, tactile reminder, beckoning you back to the process. The paper journal more readily lends itself to mind mapping, picture drawing, or creative expression. So give it a try. Buy a cool pen or two (or twelve).

The important thing is that you journal. However you want. This is your time. Commit to writing for 10 minutes a day, five days a week, for a month. Set your timer for 10 minutes and write for that whole time. Do not think about anyone else reading your journal – this is not a product that has to have correct grammar or good penmanship. This is for you and you alone. Even if you never again read what you wrote, the purpose will be served. The process of writing, working through whatever is on your mind, listing what you are grateful for, whatever it is – taking this time just for you is about finding your inner bitch and allowing her free expression.

You may find that 10 minutes is not enough. That's awesome. Keep going. But by setting the timer for 10 minutes you are allowing yourself to stop. You are setting yourself up for success, for habit formation. Over time, you will find that it becomes easier to hear what your inner bitch is saying – throughout the day, not just during your journal time. By giving her free expression for those 10 minutes, she will feel freer to voice her thoughts at any time. And you will be poised to hear her. You are training yourself to pay attention to yourself. You are getting in touch with what you want, with who you are. This is critical if you are in the early stages of finding your inner bitch. If you are in later stages, if you know who your inner bitch is and she is alive and well, journaling gives you a place to work through things together.

For the next month, commit to journaling for 10 minutes, preferably somewhere quiet where you will be uninterrupted. Set the timer on your phone, or get an hour-glass timer for 10 minutes. Then write, uninterrupted, for those 10 minutes. Refrain from judgment of any kind. Just write, or doodle if you can't think of anything to write. Draw mind maps, flow charts, clouds with your thoughts in them, whatever comes to your mind. If the timer goes off and you want to keep going, keep going. I'm excited for you as you begin this journey. Also know that journaling isn't for everyone, and if it turns out it's not your thing, something else will be your thing. And you will know it when you find it.

Unraveling

Brené Brown talks about "unraveling[17]" as a time when we are pulled toward living the life we are meant to live rather than the life we think we are supposed to live. In many ways, I have been unraveling for a while. I envision a baseball, with a core on the inside, surrounded by layers and layers of string, encased in a leather covering. The core (my inner bitch) can only be found if everything around it is unraveled.

Several years ago, while I was in a leadership program (WELP[12]), I was asked to come up with a vision statement for myself. I have often struggled with vision statements, feeling stuck before I even got started. But I felt this time was going to be different, for a couple of reasons. One, I was at a place in my life where I had taken some risks that made me both empowered and vulnerable. I had made a fairly substantial job change within the past twelve months, taking me out of my comfort zone, which was really uncomfortable, and putting me in a new environment where I had to figure out who I was in relation to others, personally and professionally, all over again. Two, we had sent 18-year-old Amanda on a gap year to Latin America by herself, where she was having an amazing time, learning about life along the way. Her courage with her life made me more courageous with mine. She is our youngest, so her traveling to another continent was quite symbolic for me as a parent.

Serendipity plays a role in everything we do. I was at the introspective place I was in because of the decisions I had made leading up to this moment. This time when I was asked for a vision statement, I took it to heart. I had several months before the vision statement was due. This felt like a gestational period, as I was literally trying to birth this vision. Sure, I could tell you what I wanted in life, but to really think about what I wanted my life to look like was different.

I started the process by looking for an image which represented the process of finding my vision. I spent some time thinking about vision. Vision is a way to see things. Merriam Webster[18] defines its multiple components: 1) the act or power of seeing; 2) the qualities of an object that allow our eyes to transmit signals to the brain via the optic nerve; 3) a supernatural appearance that conveys a revelation; 4) a thought or concept formed by the imagination; 5) manifestation to the senses of something immaterial; 6) act or power of imagination; 7) unusual discernment of foresight; 8) a lovely or charming sight; 9) a direct mystical awareness of the supernatural, usually in visible form.

Yikes! No wonder I have struggled with vision statements. The task seemed so big – so daunting. But this time, I was going to work through it, a little at a time. So, what did I do? I immediately began procrastinating creatively.

I focused on the metaphorical tools I needed to help me see my life. When I thought about how I wanted to come up with a vision statement, how I wanted to foresee my professional and personal future, I decided I needed tools to help me see. The first tool I came up with was a telescope – because I think they are really cool and they aid in observing remote objects, things that are far away. I liked this image a lot. I knew I wanted to be able to see the distant up close. But – just as I want to be able to look in the sky and see the moon with my eyes, I want to be able to look into my future and see some overarching trajectories, the galaxies not just the stars. By viewing life through a telescope, I might forget to enjoy life now because I would be focusing on and planning for the very distant future.

Next, I moved to binoculars, because they helped one see things that are far away, but closer than the galaxies. Binoculars[18] – a pair of identical telescopes mounted side-by-side and aligned to point accurately in the same direction, allowing the viewer to use both eyes when viewing distant objects. Double vision! Cool! Binoculars appealed to me more than a telescope because of the sheer distance difference. Binoculars are more like the tools in my junk drawer that will help me see an unusual bird in a tree – if I had the patience for bird watching. It may be better to not look so far into the distant future. But I still felt I was missing something in my quest for vision, for seeing what was around me and what was ahead for me.

Next, I turned to the periscope – an optical instrument for viewing objects that are above the level of direct sight or in an otherwise obstructed field of vision; used especially in submarines. I love this imagery. I do not picture myself in a submarine. Rather, I picture myself in a tree fort, trying to see above the branches and leaves that, while beautiful in themselves, are clouding my view. I definitely want to see objects in an obstructed field of vision.

I need the periscope as there are areas of my life that have an obstructed view – with layers of complexity – just like the canopy of the forest. And I could use a tool that would help me see clearly when I feel like I am underwater. It is profound that many of the visual obstructions are good and beautiful things – the ocean, leaves, and branches. There are many times in my life that I can't see clearly because I have engulfed myself in good things – too many good things that have obscured my vision of the best. The periscope will enable me to see the clarity beyond the good, the beautiful, and the complex.

And I also want to see with my naked eyes, because the nearby landscape is important. If I spend too much time looking at the horizon in a focused way, I will miss the beauty and challenges of my immediate environment. I do want to look at the ocean, leaves, and branches. I want to be able to see the obstructions for the good that they are, while also being able to see beyond them to the promise of an unobstructed life.

In the end, I decided to concentrate on my metaphorical tools of binoculars and a periscope, along with my eyes, to create my vision. I want to look at my future from slightly different viewpoints, synthesizing them into a merged view with depth. I also realized I needed a flashlight. Shining light on a situation means deliberating focusing on it – being willing to pull it out of the box and look at it. This isn't always a pleasant experience – much like cleaning out a child's backpack at the end of the school year. But turning it inside out, shining a flashlight in the corners – at least then I know what I am dealing with. The flashlight can help illuminate the darkness, making it known. The unknown is often scarier than the known.

This progression took several months of thinking, struggling to find the image that I thought represented how I would find my vision for the year. I ended up with four tools (binoculars, periscope, naked eyes, flashlight), not just one. My inner bitch and I felt equipped to begin creating my vision.

The Backpack

The tools I spent months identifying? I carry them in my backpack. Along with many other items, some of which do not belong. The backpack became my metaphor for my life.

The backpack metaphor came to me one crystal clear fall morning as I was driving to coaching training at sunrise. I was driving down the highway, headed east as the sun was coming up over the horizon. That bright sun made me realize that I needed to add sunglasses to my toolkit, because the bright light of introspection and reflection may be too painful, too real at times, making me vulnerable and perhaps even momentarily blinded. That brought all of the above to my mind – the importance of the binoculars, periscope, and flashlight – and now the sunglasses.

I needed to protect my vulnerability. I needed to provide myself protection from the glare. Shining the light in my dark crevices, illuminating my challenges, may best be accomplished with sunglasses available for when the light, though helpful, is momentarily too bright. Providing this protection allows my inner bitch to be vulnerable. Testing vulnerability is best done in safe spaces.

I was so excited about this new addition to my quest for finding my vision for my life. I pulled to the shoulder of I-40 to capture all of this on paper so I would not forget it.

I was excited, I was proud. It felt like the culmination of all that I had been working toward; I had found the final piece of the puzzle, making the picture complete. Until – on the side of the road – I searched my backpack and could not find a pen, or any other writing utensil, or any form of paper.

Really? In this giant backpack with the many pockets, there is no pen or paper?

I frantically searched the car and eventually found a crayon and a napkin under the seat. While I jotted down my inspiration, I was stunned by another, more profound realization.

I have always wanted to be a writer. I wrote as a child, I had written in journals for years, I had started a blog, I had several books in my head waiting to come out.

And I was not carrying, literally or figuratively, the tools I needed to be who I was – who I needed to be to fulfill my vision. I had spent a good portion of a year trying to come up with a visual for my search, my excavation, and I was missing what I consider to be an essential part of my inner bitch – the part that allowed me to express myself, to share my views, to be creative. Wow.

I was not making time or space in my life to become a writer. I was waiting until…. I was not being intentional.

I was deeply affected by this seemingly minor diversion to jot down a note. What was in my backpack if what I truly wanted and needed was not in there? Why was it so heavy? What, exactly, was I lugging around? The purpose of the flashlight became clear – I needed to look in the crevices of my backpack to see what was weighing me down. What baggage was I carrying that I was not consciously aware of? And how did it get there?

I spent some time that weekend examining the crevices of my metaphorical backpack. When I got home from coaching training that afternoon, I immediately put a notepad and a pen in my physical backpack, insisting I would never be without them again.

I mind mapped what was in my backpack. I realized I was carrying around a lot of unnecessary baggage and legacy luggage. I had work issues that were weighing heavily on me, causing me to lose sleep and not perform my best. I carried other people's expectations, self-doubt, tendency toward overworking and holding on to anxiety and stress, and limiting beliefs about myself, including the imposter syndrome. My responsibility strength was so strong that I accidentally wrote it down twice when I was mind mapping the contents of my backpack. I've studied Freud enough to know that was not a coincidence.

I carried good things with me as well – leadership skills, communication skills, emotional intelligence, and my other strengths of achiever, input, relator, and intellection. But when I consciously thought about what I want to carry in my backpack, I knew I needed to remove some of the weight to lighten my load as well as to make room for the items I chose to add. I wanted to add my binoculars, periscope, flashlight, and sunglasses. I wanted to include my kaleidoscope to remind me to shift and pause. I wanted to add rest and introspection, time with friends, time with family, healthy behaviors such as exercise and eating well, a good night sleep, and perhaps most importantly – a pen and paper so I could allow my inner bitch to express herself whenever she wanted.

When I think about the meaning of my backpack over my life, the symbolism is strengthened. My backpack is where I carried the food that I hid in my drawer as a child. My backpack is where I carried the candy bar during graduate school that helped me reframe my relationship with food. My backpack is my nerd pack that I carry to work, resisting the pull to carry a professional leather bag to save my back and declare my nerd-ship. If we can reclaim nerd and make it an admirable label, we can reclaim bitch in the same way. That was my thought when I labeled my inner core as my inner bitch. I am going to reclaim bitch in the same way nerd has been reclaimed.

You may not carry a real backpack like I do, but you certainly carry a metaphorical one. What is in your bag?

There may be things in your backpack you can no longer identify or have outlived their usefulness. What stories have you internalized from your childhood, or from society? Are you carrying someone else's baggage?

My backpack is a symbol for my life – it is the container for what I hold dear. It is my own Tiffany box. It is my reminder to intentionally weed out what doesn't belong in my life, as its weight grows and weighs me down. It is where I lovingly and intentionally add the things that matter most.

Pause: Packing Intentionally

Think about your backpack – both metaphorically and literally.

Let's start with your literal backpack. If you are more grown up than I and use a professional bag, it will work as well. Take a look inside your bag. Feel free to use a flashlight if you want to look in the crevices.

What is in there that you didn't realize you were carrying with you everywhere you go? You know – those old receipts or notes that you can no longer identify. What do you carry with you on a regular basis? What weighs you down? Do you have the tools that you need? Do you have what you really want in there? How much do you carry but don't actually use? Like the work files that travel back and forth from home to the office without ever being opened at home, as if the work could get done through osmosis.

When I did this exercise with some *Sol Searching* retreat participants, they identified items like gum and lip balm as items that they often wanted but didn't have. Instead they were carrying dried out pens or extra paperclips. Take some time to care for yourself by equipping your bag with what you need and want. What will make you feel nurtured? How much do you really need to carry? How much is unintentional baggage?

Let's move to your metaphorical backpack. What is in your pack? Consider how much these things weigh you down. The items in your backpack are not of equal weight. Those items that are not yours to carry weigh the most. Are you carrying other people's problems or issues? Are you carrying old stories/messages that no longer serve you?

What positive things are you carrying with you? What tools do you carry? This is an opportunity to celebrate the great things that you have with you – empathy, compassion, leadership, your strengths, and more.

Some items may fall into both categories. Responsibility and achievement, for example. Both are good, to an extent. Both can also be very weighty if allowed to grow too much. Moderation and how well they fit your needs are key. There are also times in your life when it is necessary to carry things that you may not need to carry later in life. A diaper bag, for example, is very useful when you have an infant. Not so useful when your child is 15. Taking those things out of your backpack when they are no longer needed will provide more room for things you want to carry.

Exercise: Find a picture of a backpack online. Print three copies of the picture. You can also use three black pieces of paper. On the first picture, write down the things you carry in your metaphorical backpack. I like to write the things I am carrying that I want to carry in black and the items I would like to stop carrying or minimize in red. But you do it however works for you.

On the second backpack, write the items you are not currently carrying that you would like to add. These items could come from your 'words to live by' exercise or your self-care exercise. What are you missing? Be creative, thinking about what you want to add. What tools do you want to add? What do you want to strengthen?

On the third backpack, write only those things that you consciously choose to carry in your backpack. If there are some things from the first picture that you need to keep but you want to minimize, write the word smaller. Eliminate those negative, weighty items when you can. This will make room for the tools, strengths, activities that you want to add.

You may find you come back to this exercise repeatedly, as you think of additional items you are carrying or that you want to add. Make this work for you. You also may want to revisit this exercise frequently to make sure items don't slip into your backpack and take permanent residence. Shining the flashlight in the crevices frequently can help you stay balanced.

This backpack will help guide you when you make your to-do or to-not-do list and fill your calendar. Intentionally choose your activities, your thoughts, your beliefs, your habits, and ultimately your life.

Bonus Pause: Create your Personal MBA (Mastering Bad-Assery)

An investment in knowledge pays the best interest.
– Benjamin Franklin

In our world of measurement and accomplishment, many of us pursue additional education in some form. I have recently decided that I am going to get my own personal MBA – Mastering Bad-Assery. I have created a curriculum around what I want to learn, where I want to focus, who I want to engage, and who I want to be as my full-fledged, unabashed badass with her inner bitch thriving.

We have one life – do we want to use it waiting to be our true selves – waiting until it's safe or less chaotic? Until we retire or have more time? All of those things (except retirement) happen as we establish our own sense of self. Can we have a 'lifelong retirement attitude' – cultivating the commitment to find ways to do what we want and be who we are throughout life?

Creating your personal MBA is about investing the time and resources into who you want to be. Resources could mean spending money but it can also mean finding those people who may be able to help you, teach you, and support you. But let's talk about money for a minute. We are often quick to spend money on others, especially our children if we have them. You are also worthy of your investment. Just like money invested in the stock market, an investment in you will compound over time, making it more valuable than the initial investment.

We are also willing to spend a lot of time planning our upcoming vacations. Are you worth spending the same amount of time (and possibly even more) to plan who you want to be and how you can get there?

Exercise: This is likely an ongoing exercise, at least for a little while. Think about what you want to learn, who you want to become. Think about the steps you can take, the tools you can gather, the skills you can build to earn your MBA.

Write down the courses, the books, the people, and the skills you have identified. Put down the cost, whether it is finances or time, next to the items. Think about this as an education trajectory. What do you really want or need to learn? Education is beginning to go the route of alternative styles, such as virtual and remote courses. You can be on the cutting edge by creating the curriculum for your MBA. You may decide that buying a high end journal is part of your school supply list. You may decide that you are going to invest in coaching or retreats, or a class in pottery. You are the head master. You are the decider. Spend some time understanding your goal and what you need to get there.

A word of caution. Earning your MBA is about stepping into it. I encourage you to be thoughtful about your investments into yourself – don't let the plan overcome the progress. In other words, keep your plan flexible. You may not need every course, training, or book on the list. You may gain the skills by doing. There is a balance between the learning and the doing, and you need to find what is right for you. You may find that, once you start, the doing changes the list of what you want to be learning. You may eliminate and you may add. Be creative in ways that you can gain your skills and knowledge. Remember, your MBA education needs to be targeted to you.

Chapter 7: May your Inner Bitch Thrive!

I wrote this book for me. I needed this book. I still need this book. I am intensely proud of my inner bitch – for she is the one who wrote this book. She was the brave one to step out of the rubble and the chaos to make herself heard.

As you move forward, after our discovering, excavating, releasing, and nurturing your inner bitch, you want to ensure that she continues to thrive. You have done a lot of work to find her. Don't let her shrink away. Give her water and feed her. How do we do that?

Celebrate her

Every day, celebrate your wins, no matter how big or small. Enjoy your strengths and build on them. Bolster your areas of growth through finding supports that can nurture you. Recognize your growth, such as each time you realize you are not letting your noisy roommate dictate your actions or when you make intentional choices about how you spend your time.

Acknowledge the risks you take and the steps toward joy on which you embark. Every exercise in this book leads you toward joy. Every incremental step is to be celebrated.

Celebrate your inner bitch in creative ways. Lift your arms to greet the sunrise, while listening to your anthems. Sit and watch the clouds sail by. Hold a child's hand, glowing in the knowledge that through finding and celebrating your inner bitch, you are making that child's future better as well.

Protect her

Part of finding and releasing your inner bitch is ensuring that she isn't buried again, under fear, regret, negativity, or the busyness of life. Intentionally connect with her and pay attention to the cues she offers you.

It is critical to remember that not everyone gets the privilege of seeing your vulnerability. Choose the spaces, places, and people with whom you are willing to be vulnerable. You can choose a purposeful, intentional silence, which differs from the silencing others do to us. We can choose not to share our inner selves with others if we are not feeling like the time or place is right. And by doing so, you are listening to your inner bitch and letting her express her desire for safety.

Support her

Her Tribe. Your newly excavated, shiny, sparkly inner bitch will thrive if she has additional support in the form of a tribe. This tribe can be created from different groups, but essentially you will want to find women who support you and your inner bitch. Through your exploration of yourself, you may have found new interests that have led to new friends, or you may have reignited old friendships. Or you may have been more open about your true self and facilitated conversations about your inner bitch that allowed your friends and coworkers to do the same. However you find your tribe, you want to make sure you do so. Your tribe will be a sounding board, give you reassurance, and laugh and cry with you. Together, you will declare that your inner bitches are amazing and deserve to be flaunted.

Her Coach. Coaching can be a very effective way to reach your full inner bitch potential. A coaching relationship is an interactive partnership designed to help you reach your full potential, whether personally or professionally. Coaching experience and training can vary widely, so I suggest finding an ICF (International Coaching Federation) credentialed coach. The ICF regulates coaching training and qualifications and acts as a vetting organization for coaches. Only coaches who are accredited have been through approved and rigorous training.

My coaching clients have been amazed by their growth, in relatively short amounts of time. Coaching is an investment in yourself, giving yourself the gift of time and space to tap into who you really are and what matters to you.

Her Mastermind Group. A mastermind group is designed to help you navigate through challenges using the collective intelligence and experience of others. The group meets regularly, virtually or in person, to tackle challenges and problems together. They lean on each other, give advice, share connections, and do business with each other when appropriate.

This is an intentional community, designed to maximize each individual's contribution and value received. This is a collaborative community, where everyone's ideas are valued and important. Hearing different perspectives is important when one is growing and trying to think outside of the box. Having others challenge your thought processes in a professional, thoughtful way helps you move past your limiting thoughts and beliefs.

Mastermind groups are typically not groups of friends but rather carefully crafted groups of people who have expertise in different areas, such that the coming together of the group offers a variety of strengths. They offer a combination of brainstorming, education, peer accountability, and support in a group setting to sharpen business and personal skills. Members challenge each other to set strong goals and to accomplish them through accountability. Having members of different backgrounds, experiences, and expertise facilitates thinking about situations and opportunities in ways you might not have thought about them before.

Mastermind groups are catalysts for growth in a supportive atmosphere. The group setting is a place to share your ideas, hear others' perspectives, and be challenged to move forward. You also provide the same for others so this is a mutually beneficial space.

I am creating a mastermind network so please connect with me on my website or via email so we can build a strong foundation for present and future inner bitches.

Nurture her

There are so many ways to nurture your inner bitch. This whole book is about creating an environment where she can feel free to express herself safely. Doing the exercises, reading empowering books, finding a tribe, engaging in coaching and retreats, journaling, embodying words to live by, and so on. All of these nurture your inner bitch.

In addition, be sure to engage in small luxuries on a regular basis. Buy and drink the best coffee you can afford, indulge in a few squares of really good chocolate. Don't just buy what's on sale in these areas. Eat and drink what you like. You will find quality outweighs quantity.

Exercise and take care of yourself, paying attention to your need for rest and quiet as well. Getting up and moving your body makes your mind work better, makes your body healthier, and improves your mental health. Do fun exercise when you can. Dance, play games, hike. Do what makes your heart sing. And find a community that supports your self-care.

We are more likely to continue to do things that reward us in some way. It may be an actual reward, such as a new book, or the reward may be the way you feel after engaging in healthy behavior. Pay attention to how you feel when you engage in different behaviors, including adequate sleep, good nutrition, and vigorous and fun exercise. The awareness and celebration of these positive feelings will encourage you to continue these behaviors.

Dress the way you want, particularly in ways that allow you to express yourself. If you want to be able to do a cartwheel at any moment, you may want to avoid stilettoes. My bias is that you should avoid these at all times, but if you love them, and they make you feel good – go for it! Think about how your body feels with certain clothes – too tight, too restrictive, too short, etc. When you feel good, you look good. It is hard to look good when you are tugging down on your skirt or trying to walk so your feet don't hurt.

Create an environment that allows you to thrive. Get rid of clutter if it is holding you back. Don't hold on to gifts because you feel obligated to do so. Put up pictures that inspire you. Add quotes to your working space. Get cups that make you happy. Spend the energy to think about what you like and what you don't like and then make your environment match that.

And lastly for now, be who you are – accept and even celebrate the cellulite, bulges, skinny legs, stretch marks, straight hair, curly hair, gray hair, and wrinkles that make you you. You are beautiful and unique. We are all human, and humans are physically different from each other. We don't want a bunch of people who all look alike. How boring would that be? Remember that the media uses multiple techniques with smoke and mirrors to alter people's appearances to make them look more "perfect." But we can reject that definition of perfect and accept our own – we are perfect the way we are.

Share her

You have come a long way! As your inner bitch continues to thrive, you may decide you want to connect with others who are on the same journey. Moms may want support as they parent so their daughter's inner bitch stays uncovered and shiny. Teenagers may want peer groups who care more about who they are at their core than how they look. Young adults may want guidance from those who have traversed the path and camaraderie of fellow journeyers. Women of all ages may want friends who value self-discovery and self-expression. Remember, your vulnerability is a privilege. Share it with those who earn it.

There are many ways to share your inner bitch. Share the book with others. Have a book club to discuss the exercises. Connect with other women on my website (pamelamaxson.com). Come to a *Sol Searching* retreat (see Resources).

Together we will create a revolution of women who are true to who they are, in tune with what they believe and want, compassionate, sure of themselves and their values, which allow them to more fully and generously hear others, and are living an abundant and wholehearted genuine and fulfilled life.

And we will be proud to be claim our inner bitches.

Appendices
How Your Inner Bitch Can Thrive

- Have fun.
- Laugh.
- Speak up.
- Connect with our inner selves.
- Say two things in a meeting.
- Write affirmations or life statements.
- Repeat a mantra that is meaningful to you.
- Listen to and sing along with your anthems.
- Read empowering books (See Resources).
- Listen to Ted talks, podcasts, or audiobooks. Listen to them while you are taking a walk, driving to work, cleaning your house. But remember, silence is golden as well.
- Journal.
- Trace ourselves through our past and identify consistent threads.
- Reconnect with our childlike selves. What did we like to do when we were kids? How did we have fun as a child? Can we recapture that? (Playing in the dirt, swinging high on the swings, laughing, giggling, being silly….)
- Spend at least as much time planning our lives as we do planning a trip.
- See and celebrate our own uniqueness.
- Realize that others do not think about us anywhere as much as we think they do; minimize our view of our importance in others' minds.
- Learn how to deal with money and build your own financial assets.

(Taking care of yourself financially will ensure your ability to express your inner bitch. Having your own money can help you feel empowered and secure. In a world where women are in the vast majority of those who stay home with children, it is critical that we figure out ways to educate and empower women financially. Check the Resources for recommended authors.)

- Learn to negotiate. Start small, in safe areas to build your skill.
- Feel free to state what you want in all things.
- Break the habit of deferring to others all the time.
- Practice making decisions.
- Designate time for yourself.
- Understand yourself. What makes you happy? What feeds you emotionally? Spend some time with yourself, thinking about what you like to do, what gets you excited, what makes you feel calm.
- Hang out only with those who make you feel good. Prune your life of the dead limbs or the limbs that block your light.
- Strike power poses. (Power poses make me consciously think about my own power. They help me tap into the me I want to be.)
- Engage in entertainment with powerful women characters. Books, movies, television shows all have strong female leads. Find them. Read them. Watch them. Love them.
- Get a coach.
- Join or start a mastermind group.
- Attend a retreat where you can engage in the above with other inner bitches.

*Contact me on my website to add to the list.

Words to Live By

This list has been compiled over time at the *Sol Searching* retreats. Feel free to borrow some of these words.

Joy	Sunrise	Fulfillment
Health	Dogs	Kids
Freedom	Passion	Self-respect
Security	Contentment	Whimsy
Wisdom	Power	Tears
Creativity	Avocadoes	Abundance
Love	Peace	Discovery
Chocolate	Pomegranate	Tribe
Respect	Hope	Perseverance
Music	Garden	Pause
Laughter	River	Resilience
Family	Justice	Road trips
Fulfillment	Bravery	Play
Compassion	Paint	Spontaneity
Travel	Rocks	Brilliance
Success	Pride	Clarity
Adventure	Bliss	Confidence
Lightness	Humor	Optimism
Grace	Spirituality	Home
Playfulness	Adventure	Perspiration
Community	Quiet	Radiance
Centeredness	Energy	Patience
Buoyancy	Rain	Healing
Flow	Sunshine	Exercise
Nature	Ice cream	Wellness
Thrive	Vulnerability	Water
Time	Awareness	
Space	Balance	
Spontaneity	Cherish	

Resources
Sol Searching **Retreats**

Sol Searching retreats are an opportunity for women to step into a nurturing space where they can reflect on their lives, their relationships, their goals, their selves. In addition, they can practice self-care through time at the beach, sitting pool side, or enjoying the view. During the weekend, women will explore who they are and where they want to be, looking at their life holistically.

Over the years, I have heard consistent themes from women, including figuring out what to do when they 'grow up' (regardless of their age); wanting more from life but not being sure how to define what 'more' is; wanting to optimize one's self in all areas of life (health, career/work, family, friendship, etc.); and desiring space to reflect on issues that are often submerged due to hectic schedules and others' needs. These themes appear consistently across age and life stage; they simply manifest themselves in slightly different ways.

Sol Searching helps women optimize their lives, refine their goals, and reconnect with their inner selves through coaching, retreats, and workshops.

Connect with me at pamelamaxson.com.

Books that I Love

Gifts of Imperfection
Daring Greatly
Rising Strong
Braving the Wilderness
Dare to Lead
      All by Brené Brown

Year of Yes by Shonda Rhimes

Roadmap by Roadtrip Nation, Brian McAllister, Mike Marriner, and Nathan Genhard

Designing your Life by Bill Burnett and Dave Evans

Success Principles by Jack Canfield

Carry On, Warrior
Love Warrior
      Both by Glennon Doyle

Start with Why
Find your Why
      Both by Simon Sinek

Tools of Titans by Tim Ferris

Change your Thoughts, Change your Life by Wayne Dyer

Change your Questions, Change your Life by Marilee Adams

Ask and it is Given by Esther and Jerry Hicks

Mindset by Carol Dwyck

The Miracle Morning by Hal Elrod

10% Happier by Sam Harris

Real Happiness: the Power of Meditation by Sharon Salzberg

Art of Possibility by Rosamund Stone Zander and Benjamin Zander

The Happiness Advantage: The Seven Principles of Positive Psychology That Fuel Success and Performance at Work by Shawn Anchor

Expectation Hangover by Christine Hassler

You are a Badass
You are a Badass at Making Money
      Both by Jen Sincero

Resisting Happiness by Matthew Kelly

Lean In by Sheryl Sandberg

The Dumb Things Smart People do with their Money by Jill Schlesinger

Women and Money by Suze Orman

Women with Money: The Judgment-Free Guide to Creating the Joyful, Less Stressed, Purposeful (and, Yes, Rich) Life You Deserve by Jean Chatzky

Podcasts to get you started

Jill on Money
Don't Quit your Day Job
Achieve your Goals
Oprah's Super Soul Conversations
10% Happier
Good Life Project

Notes

1. Maslow, A. H. (1943). A theory of human motivation. *Psychological Review, 50*(4), 370.

2. My interpretation of how belonging runs throughout the hierarchy.

3. Maslow, Abraham. (1954). *Motivation and Personality.* Harper and Brothers Publishing.

4. Erikson, Erik. (1980). *Identity and the Life Cycle.* W.W. Norton Publishing.

5. Elkind, D. (1967). Egocentrism in adolescence. *Child Development, 38*(4), 1025-1034.

6. Marcia, J. E. (1980). Identity in adolescence. *Handbook of adolescent psychology, 9*(11), 159-187.

7. Virginia Slims ad campaign: "You've Come a Long Way, Baby: Virginia Slims Advertising Year By Year", by Yeoman Lowbrow on October 3, 2016. https://flashbak.com/youve-come-a-long-way-baby-virginia-slims-advertising-year-by-year-365664/

8. "Develop your Life" combines developmental psychology, human development, and human-centered design with a focus on the developing human – the student. Students examine their own development to date, including influences and contextual factors, understanding their 'self' in the present and considering a plan for the future which combines the best parts of the past and the present.

9. Sandberg, Sheryl. (2013) *Lean In.* Knopf Publishers.

10. Tara Sophia Mohr, "Why women don't apply for jobs unless they're 100% qualified," August 25, 2014.

https://hbr.org/2014/08/why-women-dont-apply-for-jobs-unless-theyre-100-qualified

11. The anti-inflammatory diet involves eliminating foods which can cause inflammation in people, such as sugar, flour, and dairy. After eliminating these foods, they are added back one at a time to identify what caused inflammation for the individual. There are many resources online, if you are interested.

12. Women's Executive Leadership Program (WELP), The Impact Center. https://the-impact-center.org/womens-leadership-institute-overview-1

13. Rath, Tom. *StrengthsFinder* 2.0. https://www.gallupstrengthscenter.com

14. The story of Jim Carey and the law of attraction. https://www.applythelawofattraction.com/jim-carrey-law-attraction/

15. Brown, Brené. (2010). *The Gifts of Imperfection*. Hazelden Publishing.

16. Gallery Leather. www.galleryleather.com

17. Brené Brown, "The Midlife Unraveling," May 24, 2018. https://brenebrown.com/articles/2018/05/24/the-midlife-unraveling/

18. Merriam Webster dictionary, https://www.merriam-webster.com

Finding Your Inner Bitch

Acknowledgements

Many people played a part in bringing this book to life – and I am grateful. I want to thank my parents, first and foremost, for supporting me through everything I have chosen to do in my life. Thanks Mom and Dad – you are the rock for so many.

Brayton, Ben, and Amanda – thank you for being patient with me as I learned how to be whole while you were growing up. You were my true teachers. You taught me how to love without fear, to hold on and to let go. I'm still working on letting go. You may have to be patient with me for a bit longer. You have taught me that life is meant to be lived - and that living involves laughing until your stomach hurts, loving when others may turn away, holding out a hand when it may not be convenient, wiping away tears with a gentle touch, and finding solutions to problems, especially empowering others to make a difference in their own lives and in their community. When I look into your eyes, I see the depth of our joint experiences. I see your true selves.   And you are incredible.

Brian, we continue to grow individually and together after 32 years. We are definitely getting better with age. Thank you for being supportive of this book even though it meant I was a wee bit preoccupied for 9 months. Thank you for being my traveling buddy on my journey. Thank you, especially, for forcing me to go snowmobiling.

My tribe – so many have provided support, advice, wine, Kleenex, friendship, and encouragement. There are too many to name, but I trust you know who you are. To my editorial board, aka book mastermind group, (Amanda, Amanda, Adaora, Barbara, Barb, Bev, Brenda, Brian, Collie, Eve, Laura, Lori, Mom, Sandy, Stacey, Susan, and Vivian) – thank you for helping to make this book better. Similar to the way you have accepted me in my varying states of completeness, you readily opened your arms to my developing creation. Clare, thank you for your patience with me while we iteratively created the cover. We went full circle and back again – I enjoyed the process and I love the product!

A collective thank you to everyone who has been in my life. I am who I am because of each individual I have encountered – each child I have loved, each person with and for whom I have worked, each friend I have cherished, each student I have taught. The experiences I have had and the challenges I have overcome have added depth to my journey. I would not change a thing. My inner bitch and I are working towards an abundant and wholehearted life.

Who am I to Write this Book?

My noisy roommate asked me regularly while I was writing this book – "Who are you to write this book?" My response is that I am a woman who has experienced the life-changing excavation of my inner bitch. My professional experience complements my personal experience. My PhD in Human Development has provided me the theoretical and practical understanding of how we develop over time, amidst multiple influences. My 20+ years of undergraduate teaching, fifteen years in operational leadership, and my work in leadership and life coaching have demonstrated to me that this book is needed, across all ages. My coaching focuses on professional and personal development. I facilitate an individual's understanding of leadership style, maximizing leadership potential, goal and priority setting amidst multiple competing priorities, strength building, communication, work-life integration, and personnel development and management. In the personal realm, I partner with individuals to find their inner bitches, discover and leverage their strengths, align their goals and activities with their values, develop their best lives, manage competing priorities, engage in self-care, and more. This dichotomy between professional and personal, though, is manufactured – we live our whole lives, just in different contexts. I earned my graduate degrees from Pennsylvania State. I am still deciding what I want to do when I grow up. I am an internationally credentialed coach and enjoy leadership and life coaching. Most importantly, I am a wife of over 30 years, a mom of three young adults, a sister, a daughter, a friend, and an inner bitch excavator.

Connect with me at pamelamaxson.com.